# *The*
# PENDLE HILL
## *Reader*

# The
# PENDLE HILL
# Reader

Edited by
## HERRYMON MAURER

Introduction by
## ELTON TRUEBLOOD

*Essay Index Reprint Series*

 BOOKS FOR LIBRARIES PRESS
FREEPORT, NEW YORK

INTERNATIONAL STANDARD BOOK NUMBER:
0-8369-2415-0


LIBRARY OF CONGRESS CATALOG CARD NUMBER:
74-142668


PRINTED IN THE UNITED STATES OF AMERICA
BY
NEW WORLD BOOK MANUFACTURING CO., INC.
HALLANDALE, FLORIDA 33009

# CONTENTS

# NOTE

The material in this reader has been selected for its bearing on the solution to man's inward crisis that must come before any solution of the outward problems of war and peace, poverty and plenty. The various parts of the book have appeared separately as Pendle Hill pamphlets over a ten-year period; they have been specially edited and revised for this collection. For information on other Pendle Hill pamphlets address the Publications Secretary, Pendle Hill, Wallingford, Pennsylvania.

# INTRODUCTION

The writings included in this volume are not characteristic of our time. They are not different because they are religious, but because they are religious in unusual ways. In the first place, these modest writings may be classified, for the most part, as religious literature rather than literature about religion. We have hundreds of new books each year which are called religious, but many of them discuss religion as a matter of interest. They tell about its intellectual defense, its prospects, its dangers. The reader of the present volume will soon note that the eight essays gathered here demonstrate very little of this familiar quality. All of the authors represented seek, with varying degrees of success, to share with readers their own experiences of God. Religion, so far as this book is concerned, is not primarily something to be discussed or argued, but something to be experienced, demonstrated and shared. This is the literature of witness.

The present writings differ from the majority of current books in another way in that they are more than individual. For seven of these writers Pendle Hill is not merely an organization which has sponsored publications and not merely a school where the authors have lectured or learned; instead it is a community in which they have shared so deeply that each writer is forced to write out of the experience of sharing and not merely out of his own separated consciousness. The situation is not wholly dissimilar to that of Port Royal in the seventeenth century.

Pendle Hill is a learning and teaching community, wholly

without degrees or the ordinary educational trappings of our time. It is located in suburban Philadelphia, near the Wallingford Station, carrying on its activities in two houses and a barn. People come to Pendle Hill for longer or shorter periods to share in work, study and daily worship in the simple Quaker way. It is almost inevitable that all become committed to that kind of basic Christianity in which men and women come to know directly, rather than by mere speculation or mere tradition, the healing ministrations of the Living Christ. It is out of this shared experience that all these writings have come.

Much as Jansenists once brought out the *Port Royal Logic,* these authors have joined forces to bring out *The Pendle Hill Reader.* The names of the individual authors could have been omitted without significant loss.

All of the particular chapters have been published before as Pendle Hill pamphlets and Arnold Toynbee's lecture has also been published in a collection of his own. The present printing brings together materials which tend to become scattered when only in pamphlet form and gives strength to each by the combination.

Two of the essays will be especially moving to many sensitive readers because we do not have the privilege of hearing the voices of their authors any more. These are the essays of the late Rufus M. Jones and the late Thomas R. Kelly. A great many people in the modern world wish to know what the meaning of the Quaker Movement is and here Rufus Jones tells them. He always interpreted Quakerism as the religion of immediate experience and now his simple words express this in a way open to the understanding of any seeker:

This Quaker philosophy of life was not a speculation and it was more than a faith. It was a vivid experience. The Light from beyond actually broke in on them and flowed over all their darkness. They knew God experimentally. They felt the healing drop into their souls from under God's wings.

Like Rufus Jones, Thomas Kelly interpreted Quakerism as fundamentally *empirical*. It is not enough, he insisted, to *believe*; we must actually *experience* the love of God. There are many paragraphs in Thomas Kelly's essay which the reader may wish to underline. His words came out of what can only be called a baptism by fire. He was *enkindled* and he burned with a fast flame. Some of these words were written only a few days before his sudden death in January, 1941, when he seemed to be in the very height of his career.

Thomas Kelly, as the reader will note, was not ignorant of the conventional defenses of Christianity, nor did he despise them, but he was very sure that a deeper level of conviction is open to us. Perhaps the following paragraph will be remembered as long as any, for it states his emphasis precisely:

But there is a wholly different way of being sure that God is real. It is not an intellectual proof, a reasoned sequence of thoughts. It is the fact that men *experience* the presence of God. Into our lives come times when, all unexpectedly, He shadows over us, steals into the inner recesses of our souls, and lifts us up in a wonderful joy and peace. The curtains of heaven are raised and we find ourselves in heavenly peace in Christ Jesus. . . . In such times of direct experience of Presence, we know that God is utterly real. We need no argument. When we are gazing into the sun we need no argument, no proof that the sun is shining.

These moving words are the words of only one of the authors, but they underlie the work of all. This is the ground on which they meet and upon which they build. The ancient Quaker journals which Howard Brinton quotes were written to bear personal witness to such an experience. The experiments in fellowship which Douglas Steere describes are experiments which both arise from such immediate experience and accentuate it. It is experience of this kind which raises the concept of perfection out of the level of fruitless debate. It is this experience which brings an inner peace that is wholly compatible with a life of constant travel in the spread of the gospel. It is the living silence at the center of our lives which makes it possible to "listen on the run."

Here is a witness which may appeal to contemporary minds with a peculiar power partly because it is not characteristic of our age. It may give what the world does not give and thus help men to live more adequately in the world. True religion must always be partly out of step with the world and thus be a corrective to the world.

Though most of the writers in this volume are associated with the Quaker Movement and all have felt its influence, the book, in its general impact, is not sectarian. The Quaker experiment in basic Christianity is used often for purposes of illustration, but the words are not for the most part directed chiefly or solely to members of the Society of Friends. What is sought and advocated is religion of Christian veracity which is truly catholic in scope and which may appeal to all men everywhere, if only they will listen. The Quaker experiment is taken out of its sectarian limitations and made available to all who long for one sheepfold and one Shepherd.

In the year 1652, almost three hundred years ago, George Fox, as a young and unknown man, stood on Pendle Hill in England. Deeply sensitive to the confusion and perplexity of his time he had a vision of what he called "a great people to be gathered." He began to understand how there were multitudes of honest and perplexed seekers who were equally dissatisfied with conventional religion and with conventional irreligion. As we look now from our modern hilltop we may be sure that this is even more widely true in the modern situation. How can these restless seekers be found and reached? Perhaps this book is part of the answer.

ELTON TRUEBLOOD

*May, 1950*

*The*

PENDLE HILL

*Reader*

# I

# THE REALITY OF THE SPIRITUAL WORLD

*Can this be the love of God, this burning, tender, wooing, wounding pain of love that pierces the marrow of my bones and burns out old loves and ambitions? God experienced is a vast surprise.*

THOMAS R. KELLY

Driven for many years of his life to increasingly strict and intense scholarship, Thomas R. Kelly studied and taught philosophy at many colleges and universities, among them Earlham, Harvard, Haverford. Given not only to scholarship but to social and religious service at home and in Europe, Thomas Kelly suffered periods of uncertainty, doubt, ill health, and nervous fatigue. And then at the age of 44, three years before his death in 1941, his being was fused together by the fire of profound inward experience. What he wrote and said thereafter had in it the same exact scholarship, but it had also the stamp of authentic religious experience. This stamp is set unmistakably upon *A Testament of Devotion*, published by Harper & Brothers in 1941, and *The Reality of the Spiritual World*, lectures given at Pendle Hill during the winter of 1940-41.

How can we be sure that God is real, and not just a creation of our wishes? We have disquieting desires for a God, for a real God. There come to us times of loneliness when we seem to have a premonition of a deep vastness in ourselves, when the universe about us, gigantic in its starry depths, seems cramped and narrow for our souls, and some-

1

thing makes us long for an abiding home. We have times of fatigue, of confusion, of exhaustion, of utter discouragement, when we long for a serene and everlasting bosom on which to lay our heads and be at peace. But how can we be sure that what we call God is not a product of our wishful thinking, a self-delusion we create, a giant shadow of our longings flung up against the sky and asserted to be real?

We have moments when we long, not for freedom and yet more freedom, but for self-surrender, self-dedication, self-abandonment in utter loyalty to an Overself. If I could find an object worthy of my utmost allegiance, if I could find a mark worthy to be the aim of the bow of my life, I should gladly pull the arrow back to its head and let all fly upon a single shot. I should be integrated, freed from internal conflicts, those confusions and tangles within which make me ineffective, indecisive, wavering, half-hearted, unhappy. I should gladly be a slave of such a being, and know that I am truly free when I am his utter slave. But I have seen men and women, my brothers and sisters in Germany and Italy and Russia, who joyfully commit their all to the state, to an earthly state which to them seems noble, glorious, and ideal. They seem to get integration and joy in enslavement similar to that which my religious friends get from commitment to an invisible, spiritual world. Maybe the values all lie on the subjective side, on the integration of self and the dedication of will to *any* object which is conceived as worthy. Maybe the object doesn't have to be real but just thought to be real with a vigorous, fanatical intensity. I know that false ideas and misplaced enthusiasms have had as real effects upon men and upon history as have well-grounded beliefs and ideals. Maybe the whole conviction of a spiritual reality shadowing over us all is such a hoax, a useful hoax as long as we believe it intensely, a hoax that stabilizes men and society and one that ought to be preserved and nourished and fostered for its useful social effect.

But there is an inner integrity in us all which rejects all programs of *as if*. We cannot merely act *as if* there were a God, while we secretly keep our fingers crossed. This inner integrity demands the *real*; we cannot long tolerate complex ways of kidding ourselves, nor forever whistle to keep our courage up. It is an old maxim, with a double meaning: "Let the truth be known, though the heavens fall." We are such creatures as demand to build upon the Truth. And if the Truth is that there are no heavens, but only earth, no real God, but only human cravings for a God, then we want to know *that*, and adjust our lonely lives to that awful fact.

*First Argument: Analogy*

Caught in this difficulty—that we long for a real God, no, demand a real God, yet can be sure only of our subjective longings, not of God's objective existence—we ask a devout friend, "Are you sure that God is real?" And he replies, "Yes, I am absolutely sure." We then continue, "But why are you so sure there is a reality, an actually existent reality corresponding to your religious cravings?" He replies, "I find myself in a world which furnishes real objects to answer all my central cravings. In me, subjectively, there is a craving for food. And I find, out there, in the world, that the Universe furnishes me real food. In me I find a profound craving for companionship. And out in the world there are real men and women who give their fellowship in answer to my craving. In me is an insistent craving for sex. And I find myself set in a Universe that furnishes real beings of the opposite sex. I find in myself a craving for beauty, and out there I find beautiful objects that satisfy my soul. And when I find in myself a profound craving for God, for an absolute resting place for my soul's devotion, an object for my last loyalty, I believe that here, too, there is an answering object. The same structural situation—subjective craving, satisfying Object— is to be expected."

"But," we answer, "you are arguing from analogy. And analogies are notoriously treacherous. You argue that the fact of food-hunger, with its answering object of real food, gives you the right to say, 'From the fact of God-hunger I am sure there is a real bread of life.' But analogies break down. If analogies were always perfect, they would cease to be analogies and become identities. No, the time comes when similar situations part company, and are different. Perhaps the matter of God's real existence is just such a case. One can't be sure. *And I want to be sure.* At best your argument from analogy only indicates the possibility that there is an objectively real God, corresponding to my hunger for Him. Perhaps it even indicates *probability*. But I want deeper grounds than that."

## Second Argument: Authority

Disappointed in this first argument for the reality of a spiritual being wherein we may cradle our life, we turn in a second direction and ask a devout Protestant: "Do you believe that God is utterly real?" He replies, "Yes," and you ask, "Why?" To which he answers, "The Bible tells me God is real, that in Him we live and move and have our being." "But why do you believe the Bible?" To this he replies, "Because the Scriptures are inspired." You reply, "Yes, I strongly agree with you. But I suspect you and I may mean different things. Why do you say Scripture is inspired? Is it because you find in it the record of men who were drinking from the same fountains of life that well up in you, so that you, too, could write inspired words that would feed other hungry souls?" "Oh, no, no," he might hastily reply, "I am no such great soul. God chose special men to write the Scriptures, and I'm not one of them." To this you may reply, "I disagree, and am bold enough to believe that the fountains of inspiration are not stopped. There is no one age of inspiration, no one special class of inspired. Either divine inspiration is renewed in every age and in all peoples, or it never flowed at all. Now tell me, why do you believe the Bible is inspired so that you can rely upon its testimony to the reality of God?" He answers, "The Bible is inspired because it is written, 'All Scripture is given of God.' " "But wait. Do you mean to prove the Bible by the Bible? That is the crudest circle in argument. By the same argument the Book of Mormon is inspired, for it says it is, and therefore you must believe all Mormon teachings." Then he retreats and says, "But the Bible is an ancient and revered authority, tested by time, canonized by Councils, and believed by multitudes." You answer, "So are the Buddhist scriptures, such as the *Dhammapada* and *The Lotus of the Wonderful Law.* Your argument only amounts to this, 'Forty million Frenchmen can't be wrong.' You only argue, 'Forty million or forty billion Christians can't be wrong in trusting the Bible.' But if you ask forty million Asiatics you'll get a different answer. You'll have to surrender the authority of the Bible if it is based upon the circular argument, 'The Bible is authoritative because it says authoritatively that it is authoritative.' After which you can't retreat into the argument, 'The Bible is a good and reliable authority because masses of people believe in it,' imposing as that fact is. Mass agreement, even upon the existence of God, is not enough to prove that God exists. Maybe the whole of mankind is deluded on the matter. That's just my problem. And you don't settle it for me by appealing to the authority of a revered Book, if that authority is guaranteed only by mass acceptance."

The authoritarian evidence for the reality of God as given by many Protestants, who make the Book the supreme authority, reappears in different form if an average Roman Catholic is approached. His final defense of the authority of the Bible might be that the Holy Church guaranteed the reliability of the Bible and the widespread conviction that there is a really existent God. For did not the Church Fathers and the Councils and the Bible agree in this matter, that there is a God in heaven, brooding over the world in love? But long ago Abelard startled the Roman Church by printing a little book with each page in two columns, in which, without comment, he set side by side contradictory statements of the Fathers of the Church. Evidently authorities disagree. And when authorities disagree, who shall be the authority to choose between authorities? Roman Catholics would reply, "The Pope is infallible when he officially makes a decision." But you ask, "Who guarantees the infallibility of the Pope?" Answer: "The Vatican Council in 1870 pronounced the Pope infallible." But are Church Councils infallible, so that they can infallibly guarantee the infallibility of the Pope? No, only the Pope is infallible. And there you are with authoritarian guarantees of the reality of God fallen to the ground.

### Third Argument: Causation

I shall take time to state only one more effort to prove the objective reality of the spiritual world. For, honestly, all these arguments leave me cold. Even if they were sound—and none of them is watertight—they would only quiet my intellectual questionings. They would never motivate me to absolute dedication to Him for whom I yearn. But religious men are dedicated men, joyously enslaved men, bond servants of God and of his Christ, given in will to God. Arguments are devised subsequent to our deep conviction, not preceding our conviction. They bolster faith; they do not create it.

The third argument is this: Here is a world, amazingly complex, astonishingly interknit. Here are flowers, depending upon bees for pollination, and bees dependent upon flowers for food. Yonder are the heavens, adjusted, maintained, wheeling their way through staggering spaces in rhythm and order. Whence comes it all, if not from God? And here am I, a complex being, of amazing detail of body and astounding reaches of mind. Yet my parents didn't *make* me; they are as incapable of being my true cause as I am incapable of being the true cause of my children. This whole spectacle is too vast, too well articulated to be caused by any single thing *in* the world. There must be a cause outside and beneath the whole, which I call God, who creates, maintains, and preserves the whole world order.

Such an argument seems imposing and appealing to us all. But it is not absolutely watertight. For notice, this is not a perfect world, as we all know only too well from observation and experience. There are imperfections and flaws in it, notes that jar as well as notes that blend. The argument rests upon only half the evidence, the good in the world, not the evil and dislocation. There are maladjustments as well as adjustments. We may marvel at the human eye. But the physicist Helmholtz said that if an optical workman made for him an apparatus as imperfect and inefficient as a human eye, he would dismiss him. Here is the point: You can't argue from an imperfect effect, the world, to a perfect cause, God. An imperfect effect can only legitimately imply an imperfect cause, not a perfect one. If a world Cause made this world, He was not omniscient, but had a streak of stupidity in Him, to have allowed flaws to creep in. Or else, if He was omniscient, He was not omnipotent, for, knowing what would be a world without flaws, He couldn't produce it. Again, if He was omniscient and omnipotent, but still made an imperfect world, then He was not omnibenevolent but malicious, and delighted in torturing His creation by creating men with dreams of perfection, yet tantalizingly setting them in a world that grinds out the dreams of their hearts.

And David Hume, knowing all this, added the suggestion, maybe the world is the result of a superhuman but not divine creator who used trial and error and bungled many worlds before he succeeded in making this one. Look at a modern ocean liner, amazingly compact and interdependent, seeming to imply a master mind behind it. And then be introduced to the shipbuilder, who may be a very mediocre person, just a man like ourselves. He merely inherited the experience of repeated shipbuilders over the centuries, each of whom was no master mind but just found out a little detail and added it to the heritage. Maybe the world-Creator is stupid and bungling, but given sufficiently repeated trials and errors He may turn out a fairly decent world.

### Other Arguments Indicated

I shall not complete the list nor state the ontological argument, which argues from the notion of a perfect being involving its existence. Nor shall I state the moral argument, which argues that moral experience requires a God for its final validation. Nor shall I state the argument from the agreement of the race, from the universality of religion among all tribes of men, for I have referred to it already in pointing out that mass agreement cannot back up any belief in an authority.

But there is a wholly different way of being sure that God is real. It is not an intellectual proof, a reasoned sequence of thoughts. It is the fact that men *experience* the presence of God. Into our lives come times when, all unexpectedly, He shadows over us, steals into the inner recesses of our souls, and lifts us up in a wonderful joy and peace. The curtains of heaven are raised and we find ourselves in heavenly peace in Christ Jesus. Sometimes they come in the hour of worship, when we are gathered into one holy presence who stands in our midst and welds us together in breathless hush, and wraps us all in sweet comfortableness into His arms of love. In such times of direct experience of presence, we know that God is utterly real. We need no argument. When we are gazing into the sun we need no argument, no proof that the sun is shining.

This evidence for the reality of God is the one the Quakers primarily appeal to. It is the evidence upon which the mystics of all times rest their testimony. Quakerism is essentially empirical; it relies upon direct and immediate experience. We keep insisting: It isn't enough to *believe in* the love of God, as a doctrine; you must *experience* the love of God. It isn't enough to believe that Christ was born in Bethlehem, you must experience a Bethlehem, a birth of Christ in your hearts. To be able to defend a creed intellectually isn't enough; you must experience as reality first of all what the creed asserts. And unless the experience is there, behind it, the mere belief is not enough.

We must therefore examine this evidence from experience of God with some care, to see if it is sound, for it is crucial.

First, let us notice that this experience which seems so clearly to be an experience of God energizes us enormously, in a way far different from arguments. Arguments that convince our intellect alone leave us merely with questions answered, but they do not bring us to humble, joyful submission into His hands of all that we are. They do not bring the unutterable joy that makes Paul and Silas sing hymns at midnight in prison. Even though moments of the experience of presence may dawn upon us, and then fade, we are thereafter new men and women, plowed through to our depths, ready to run and not be weary, and to walk and not faint. We love God with a new and joyous love, wholly and completely. It is no commanded love, it is the joyful answer of our whole being to His revealed love. Our will becomes dedicated, our self-offering to God is vitalized by deep emotional reinforcement. I believe the real vitality of religion rests upon the fact that religious experience is universally taking place. It is not creeds that keep churches going, it is the dynamic of God's life, given in sublime and intimate moments to men and women and boys and girls.

Second, let us notice that the experience seems to come from beyond us. It doesn't seem to be a little subjective patch in our consciousness. It carries a sense of objectivity in its very heart, as if it arose from beyond us and came in as a revelation of a reality out there. If I may use a philosophic term, it is realistic. Just as my experience of that wall out there does not seem to be a subjective state of my mind, but a disclosure of a real wall out there beyond me, so the experience of God has in its inner nature a testimony that an object is being disclosed to us. We do not make it, we receive it. God seems to be the active One, we the receptive ones. And in glad discovery we know that God is dynamically at work in the world and at work in us, pressing in upon us, knocking at the door of our minds and doing things to us which arise in His own initiative.

Third, let us notice that, for the person who experiences these apparent invasions, there is set up a state of certainty about God which is utterly satisfying and convincing to himself. It is not the certainty that follows upon a sound argument. It is different, a kind of self-guaranteeing certainty. It cannot be transferred to anyone else, but it is a certainty which is enough to convince oneself completely. St. Augustine says that after such experiences he was certain of God, but *in a new way*. Intellectual convincement of the reality of God is utterly different from the felt reality of God. One may have been intellectually convinced of God's existence, but the experience of God brings a new kind of meaning to the reality of God. He is real with a vividness and an indubitableness that is powerfully overwhelming to the individual.

That inner certainty cannot be conveyed to another; it may only be caught by a contagion, as others see our lives and gain some intimation of the very springs of our being.

Now that we have given recognition to the testimony of experience, let us become more critical and intellectual. From a critical, intellectual point of view I believe that the testimony of mystic experience is not absolutely logically free from flaws. Just as all logical proofs for God's existence can be questioned, so the experiential evidence is not intellectually watertight, and we may as well face it and be aware of it. Yet I do not find my faith in the reality of the experience of God shaken by the fact that I can find intellectual holes in the testimony, any more than I find my faith shaken by discovering that all logical proofs for God's existence are defective. Such defects do not prove that God does not exist. They only drive us back to the old, old truth: we walk by faith and not by sight. Let us then be bold enough to face and acknowledge such criticism of the testimony of religious experience.

First, mere internal pressure of certainty does not prove certainty. Intense inner assurance that something is so does not make it so. The insane hospitals are full of people who have intense internal certainties that they are Jesus Christ, or Napoleon, or an angel from heaven. Shall we reject the internal pressure of certainty of the insane and keep the internal certainties of the sane? Medieval monks were internally certain that Satan whispered in their ear. If we accept some internal certainties, we should accept all, or else find some way of distinguishing between internal certainties. Not all can be true, or the world is a madhouse of contradictory certainties. I am persuaded that my experience of the presence of God is real, utterly real, that it originates in the invading love of God. But I must admit that, intellectually, my feeling of convincement is no more real and intense and, on this basis, no more reliable than the convincement of many people with whom I wholly disagree.

Second, if we retreat from this ground of assurance, we take refuge in a second assurance that our experience of God is grounded in a real God. This second assurance comes from the fact that lives that have experienced God as vividly real are new lives, transformed lives, stabilized lives, integrated lives, souls newly sensitive to moral needs of men, newly dynamic in transforming city slums and eradicating war. By their fruits we know that they have been touched, not by diaphanous visions, but by a real living power. The consequences of the experience are so real that they must have been released by a real cause, a real God, a real Spiritual Power energizing them.

This pragmatic test, this pointing to the *fruits* of religious experience, is the most frequent defense of its validity. All writers on the subject make use of it. And it is very convincing.

But there is a logical defect in this pragmatic test. Be patient with me while I turn logician for a moment. The argument runs:

> If God has really visited us, He has transformed our
>     lives.
> Our lives are transformed.
> Therefore He has visited us.

There is a patent logical fallacy in this argument, which is named the "fallacy of affirming the consequent." A valid form would be that of affirming the antecedent, and would go like this:

> If God has really visited us, He has transformed our
>     lives.
> He has visited us.
> Therefore He has transformed our lives.

But this form is of no use to us, for the minor premise, "He has really visited us," is just the question; it cannot appear as a premise but should appear in the conclusion. The only valid form in which "He has really visited us" can appear in the conclusion is in the negative form:

> If God has really visited us, He has transformed our lives.
> Our lives are not transformed.
> Therefore He has not really visited us.

But this valid argument does not prove what we were after, namely that God is really present when lives are transformed. It only proves the very important negative: He is not really present where lives are still shabby and unchanged.

But, if religious experience cannot be proved to be entirely reliable by the pragmatic argument, is religion alone in this respect? Far from it. I would remind you that the whole of experimental science which we revere today rests upon such argument and faces the same predicament. Every scientific theory that is supported by experimental evidence rests upon the fallacy of affirming the consequent. The outcome is that the whole of scientific theory is probable only, not absolutely certain. But this fact has not paralyzed science, which proceeds all undisturbed by the logical defect and, with open mind, lets down its faith upon its findings. For science rests upon faith, not upon certainty.

And this is the ground of religion. It rests upon a trust and a faith that for the religious man have become his deepest certainty, the certainty of faith, not the certainty of logic. The certainties of logic leave our wills untouched and unenslaved. Be not disturbed by the intellectual criticism of subjectivity and of mystic experience which I have given. I am persuaded that God is greater than logic, although not contrary to logic, and our mere inability to catch Him in the little net of our human reason is no proof of His non-existence, but only of our need that our little reason shall be supplemented by His tender visitations, and that He may lead and guide us to the end of the road in ways superior to any that our intellects can plan. This is the blindness of trust, which walks with Him, unafraid, into the dark.

## The Spiritual World

It may seem as if I have been kicking over a great deal of religious furniture, offering criticisms not only of the traditional proofs for God's existence but also of the validity of the mystical experience of the presence of God. But I was only doing what the great philosopher, Immanuel Kant, said he must do—destroy reason in order to make room for faith.

James Bissett Pratt of Williams College traces religious development through three stages. The first stage, primitive credulity, is found in children and in primitive peoples. The second is the stage of doubt and criticism, and is found in the years of adolescence and in sophisticated brain-worshippers. The third, the stage of faith, is reached by those who have left behind their childish belief in a big, kind man in the sky, have passed safely through the tangles of expanded intellectual vision which science, history, psychology, and philosophy give us, and have found a serene and childlike faith that stands firm in the midst of changing intellectual views. This third stage is strikingly akin to the first. It is the child-like simplicity of the truly great souls; of such, not of complicated professors, is the kingdom of heaven. It is a simplicity which is not naïve but enriched by a background of complex knowledge, not burdened or blinded by that complexity but aware of it and sitting atop it. If it has been given to you to attain this third mature stage of faith, you can voyage at will into arguments and discussions that are blasting at the second stage and be untouched by them, for your

life is down deep upon a rock that is not founded upon
argument and criticism and dispute. At this stage one can
differ radically with another person intellectually, yet love
him because he too is basically devoted to feeding upon the
bread of life and not primarily devoted to chemical analysis
of that bread.

But turning to the whole subject, the reality of the spiritual world, we may ask by whom is the spiritual world peopled? Up to this time I have been speaking only of God.
And, after all, only God matters. When men the world over
reach up to that which is highest above them, it is for God
that they yearn, no matter how He may be conceived,
whether He be Allah or Brahma or the Tao or Ahura Mazda
or the Father in Heaven of the Christian. But men have
variously peopled the spiritual world with more than God;
some have added angels, whole fluttering multitudes of
angels; some have added devils or the Devil, Satan; some
have added the souls of the departed. Some have made two
spiritual worlds, a Heaven and a Hell, with presiding divin-
ities over each. Some have split the Christian deity into a
Trinity of persons, the Father, the Son, and the Holy Ghost.
Some, like Meister Eckhart and Jacob Boehme, the greatest
mystics of the West, have asserted an Urgrund, a Godhead, a
basic view of reality underlying all the variety of divine
forms that are conceivable.

And, again, how does the spiritual world behave toward
us? Some say it is aloof, self-contained, not noticing this
world, like the gods of Epicurus and Lucretius, who, being
perfect—by definition—could not want anything, and would
be wholly unconcerned for us, not caring for our prayers,
not desiring adoration, not insulted or grieved by our sins.
Others say that God and all His angels bend over us in loving solicitude, tenderly calling us back toward our true
home, that God knocks on the doors of our hearts and whis-

pers promptings toward Himself, that He assigns guardian angels to each of us, and that He came to earth and died on Calvary on our behalf.

In the midst of this welter of views about the spiritual world, how shall we find our way? They cannot all be true insights, for some of them are mutually inconsistent. What criterion can we use for rejecting some and accepting others?

Let us try one criterion—inner experience. This was George Fox's final discovery. All outward helps he tried— preachers, reputedly great religious men—until at last, when all outward helps had failed, he turned within and found an inward teacher, the inner, living Spirit of Christ, who led him into Truth. This inward teacher of Truth is the Inner Light, the Seed of God, through whose germination within we are led into Truth.

Thus, if I experience the love of God, feeling it bathing me, brooding over me, opening up to me deep responses, and sending me out into the world of men with a new and vital love for God and man, then I can say that I know experientially that God is a loving being.

If, on the other hand, I have no experience of the Holy Trinity, if I have no direct opening whereby I know how God the Father begets the Son, and how the Holy Ghost proceeds from the Father and the Son, I let the whole Trinitarian view alone, as something not grounded in my experience.

But this test, because of its very privacy and uniqueness, would allow each individual's insights to be final, if taken alone. A religious anarchy of private opinion would result, each man being the final measurer of truth. This would be the religious analogue of the Sophists of ancient Greece, and the same sophistry is widely current today, for we find plenty of people who say, "What is true and right for me is true and right for me, and what is true and right for you is true and right for you." The public, universal character of Truth would disappear. All religious groups like the Quakers, which put the final authority not on an outer standard, but on an inner authority, must face this difficulty.

But, you may reply, if God or the heavenly order is the originator of my inner persuasions, if all men are taught within themselves by the same light and source and teacher, all men ought to agree. Maybe the wide variation in inner convictions indicates that there is no objective content to religion, only subjective wishes various in various men.

I would answer in this way: All knowing arises in a relation between two things, the object out there, and the knowing subject, the knowing person here. Our knowledge of the object is conditioned, in part, by the actual nature of the object. But it is also conditioned, in part, by the expectations, the convictions, the already settled persuasions of the knower. Experience does not deliver to us a finished, unmodified account of the object. When a criminal is in hiding, he hears a creaking board as the footstep of a pursuer. When three people testify as to what they saw in an automobile accident, the mechanic will report one thing, the housewife another, and the young man in the throes of his first love yet another. And all three are honest.

When a good Catholic like Joan of Arc has a mystical opening, she reports that St. Catherine is speaking to her. But when a Mahayana Buddhist reports a heavenly visitation, he says that Kwan Yin or Manjusri has visited him. The already accepted and dominant system of ideas in the background of the mind of the experiencer is an active modifier of the report. It is well-nigh impossible to get experience in the raw. Whatever it is in the raw, it is instantly caught up into a scheme of interpretation already pervading the mind of the experiencer. I have never heard of authentic accounts of a

Buddhist who had not read a word of Catholic theology being visited by St. Catherine or a Catholic who had never read a word about Mahayana Buddhism being visited by Manjusri. The vast cultural background in which each of us is immersed sets a broad pattern of expectation and furnishes the material for interpretation, into the texture of which whatever we might call raw experience is instantly and unconsciously woven. And the special circles of ideas in which we move do the same thing. A Quaker immersed in Quaker literature, Quaker silence, Quaker service, will reflect these things in his reports of his inner experience. On a humbler scale, anyone who reads medical books describing the symptoms of a variety of diseases is likely to find the symptoms of bubonic plague, gout, manic-depressive insanity, and tuberculosis in himself.

Rufus Jones points out that mystical experience, indeed religious experience in general, is peculiarly open to suggestion. In this he is reiterating the same fact. Suggestion that there is something to hear if one listens for echoes and messages and intuitions arising from another world will put us into a state of expectation and of listening which I believe is greatly needed, and which is facilitated by repose, silence, and the quieting of the senses. What one hears in this inward listening will be clothed in the system of ideas already current in the mind.

But, you may ask, does not inner experience bring surprises, as Joan of Arc was surprised that St. Catherine should visit her, a humble peasant girl of Domremy, and lay on her the burden of freeing France and crowning the French king? Yes, I reply, there are surprises of this sort and a certain specific crystallizing of infinite possibilities around one solution that I do not fully understand.

Take the case of Paul on the Damascus road, struck down

by the vision. He cries out, "Who art thou, Lord?" Do you think that was a genuine inquiry? By no means. He evidently had been accumulating annoying misgivings about the Christians ever since he held the men's coats at the stoning of Stephen. These misgivings, these promptings had led him to feel that maybe the living God was in these Christ-followers whom he persecuted with such zealous cruelty. They had been thrust out of the focus of his conscious life, yet remained as a submerged system of possible interpretation. Finally, in pent-up pressure, comes this moment of disclosure of the ever-present, loving Deity, and the man knows who is visiting him. The question, "Who art thou, Lord?" is purely rhetorical.

It seems clear to me that some of the surprise elements in inner experience can be interpreted in terms of repressions which are released and do genuinely seem surprising to the individual who had supposed that his daily round of conscious life and beliefs was the whole of him.

But there is another kind of surprise. One may have said all one's life, God is love. But there is an experience of the love of God which, when it comes upon us and enfolds us and bathes us and warms us is so utterly new that we can hardly identify it with the old phrase, God is love. Can *this* be the love of God, this burning, tender, wooing, wounding pain of love that pierces the marrow of my bones and burns out old loves and ambitions? God experienced is a vast surprise. God's providence experienced is a vast surprise. God's guidance experienced is a vast, soul-shaking surprise. God's peace, God's power: the old words flame with meaning or are discarded as trite, and one gropes for new more glorious ways of communicating reality. Then the subjective moulds of expectation are broken down, discarded, made utterly inadequate, as the object, God, invades the subject, man, and opens to him new and undreamed of truths. For I believe there is an extension of our knowledge of God given in inner experience which goes far beyond the limits that the subjective factors of expectation and suggestibility can account for. The new wine must be put into new wineskins lest all be lost. We become new creatures, new in intellectual moulds, new in behavior patterns, new in friendships and conversations and tastes, as the experience of God breaks down the old, inadequate, half-hearted life-moulds of religion and of conduct.

Then we find an answering test in the group, which fortifies our inner experience. We find that some other people, perhaps saintly persons whom we had scorned a little, as over-pious or over-zealous know the same thing that has come to us. We find that some quiet, unnoticed Friends know it. They had not attracted our attention before, for we had formerly had a pattern of importance in terms of people's executive ability or shrewdness in business or soundness and sanity in worldly judgments. But *now* we find that we have a new alignment of recognition of important souls, and a powerful drawing toward those who have tasted and handled the word of life. This is the fellowship and communion of the Saints, the blessed community.

We find a group answer in the Scriptures. For now we know, from within, some of the Gospel writers and the prophets and the singers of songs. They are now seen to be singing our song, or we can sing their song, or the same song of the Eternal Love is sung through us all and out into the world. In mad joy we reread the Scriptures for they have become new. They are a social check upon our individual experience, not as a law book, but as a disclosure of kindred souls who have known a like visitation of God.

After this consideration of the checks we need in examining our inner intuitions and experiences, we come back to the question: Who people the unseen world?

Let us first accept, without further discussion, God as the prime inhabitant.

I would not add a second god, the Devil, to the world of spiritual reality. I have never experienced the Devil as a spiritual being, but that doesn't decide it. Others have; Martin Luther even threw an ink bottle at him. But I still don't believe in the Devil as a second, black god. I have even seen his hoofmark on a stone wall in Nuremberg, in Germany, but I still don't believe in the Devil. I read in the Bible about the Devil, yet I am unconvinced. George Fox talks freely about the Devil, but I am not impressed. I believe the Devil was devised to account for the evil and maladjustment in our world. An early effort to explain our world led men to divide the world's double aspect of good and evil into two parts and assign each to a separate ruler. That seemed to save God from responsibility for evil, a problem that is acute if you have only one God. But I cannot think that God and the Devil could work together in such close co-operation as would be required of them if they made the world jointly, God doing the good part, the Devil doing the bad part. On God's side, God would have had to be defective if He did it in this way. He was not very powerful if He could not stop the Devil from putting his fingers into the creation process. Or He was not very good; otherwise He would not have made so many concessions to the Devil in the process. And on the Devil's side, the Devil would lose his real badness and his hostility to God, if he cooperated so nicely with the good as would be required. He ceases to be a bad devil, and becomes a benevolent, docile, co-operative spirit, really good at heart, and not too bad to have around the house. Anyway, the history of the devil idea as it appears in the Bible and in the medieval Church is fairly clear. It came from Persia, from the Zoroastrian faith, and seeped across into Asia Minor and crept into Christian tradition as an alien element from the outside, not an indigenous development.

I would not add to the unseen world an array of angels, a multitude of the heavenly host praising God and saying, "Glory to God in the highest, and on earth peace to men who are of good will." I know that the Bible reports such a population in heaven, with occasional visits to earth on some celestial commission. But the Bible reports that demons went out of the Gadarene demoniac and entered into a drove of pigs and made them run into the lake and cause extensive property damage to the owner. Antiquated medical views of Palestine regarding the nature of insanity need not be binding upon us, any more than Egyptian modes of dream interpretation, reported in Genesis or Daniel, are binding upon us. And I find no greater necessity to accept a multitude of good spirits than of bad demons.

I know, too, that many people report *experiencing* the angels in inner intuition and in visions. But I have always felt sure that God Himself could deal directly with my soul, without sending any intermediaries. In fact, one of my joys as a Quaker is in the removal of all the earthly apparatus of mediation between me and God, and I should find small comfort in discovering that, on the other side of this world, the whole array of intermediaries is duplicated. No matter how benevolent such beings might be, I long for God, not for them. To my mind, angels represent the vestigial remains of a multitude of gods softened by the idea of a monarchy. The time was when all the multitude of functions of God was accounted for by setting up a separate deity for each function. By and by, as the world grew older and more ripe, the unity of God's nature brought all these separate strands, formerly thought to be separate beings, into the coverage of the one being, God. The system of angels represents an intermediate stage in this growth from true polytheism to complete monotheism. The actual luxuriant growth of angels in the medieval Church has a definite historical route of entry.

They, too, came originally from Persia, from the Zoroastrian dualism of God and Devil, with a lot of intermediate, competing spirits organized into two armies and competing on earth for the souls of men. A neo-Platonic writer of the Fifth Century A.D. who came under this influence wrote a book called *The Celestial Hierarchies,* which was translated into Latin about 850 by an Irish monk named John Scotus Erigena, and the whole Pandora's box of angels got root in an age that was intellectually and religiously credulous.

I have spoken of angels as vestigial remains of polytheism when the process of movement toward monotheism was arrested at a monarchical stage. But whenever men come into a stage of belief that God is exceedingly lofty, high, transcendent, utterly removed from this low and degraded world, they insert an array of intermediaries to bridge the gap. This was peculiarly the case in the centuries beginning with the days of Jesus. God's transcendence was emphasized, His immanence minimized. The Gnostic menace to the early church involved the insertion between God and man of some thirty stages of descending degrees of glory from God toward man. They put in the God of the Old Testament as one of these intermediaries and Jesus as another, down near the bottom of the scale. I do not mean that everyone now who believes in angels emphasizes the transcendence of God at the expense of His immanence. But the creative epochs of angelology came in days of belief in excessive transcendence. And the whole layout of subangels and superangels doing the heavenly bidding is present in our literature, furnishing a pattern of suggestion for sincere mystics. Suggestion and expectation, along with the element of surprise which I have already discussed, seem to me adequate to account for the sincere, but as I see it not reliable, reports of angel visitation.

As to the departed spirits of men, now inhabiting the unseen world, there are two problems, first of their existence, and second of their efforts to take part in the earthly life which they have left behind.

The bare existence of life after death is a giant problem, needing a whole series of discussions. I shall only say that on strict, rational grounds, such as we used above, there is no inescapable waterproof demonstration that there is a life after death, any more than there is a strict watertight demonstration that God exists. It seems to me plausible to believe there is a life after death. For, as William James puts it, when I reach the time for dying, I am just beginning to learn how to live. There would be a moral absurdity in a universe that built up with such care beings who, through toil and tribulation and victory, achieved a degree of value and of promise, only to strike them on the head at the end of three score years and ten.

The second question, the activity of departed spirits and efforts on their part to get through to us with messages, I can touch only by a personal statement of attitude. I suppose the logic of the situation makes people think it plausible. If someone very much concerned with you dies, and if he retains his personal traits after death, he would still be concerned with you and would try to continue the life-sharing with you that he knew on earth. This provides a logical ground for expecting the dead to communicate with us. The other consideration which spiritualism offers is the report that some people actually experience visits and get messages from the dead. My own attitude is that of rejecting, lock, stock, and barrel the whole array of experiences of seances and mediumship as evidences of the existence and activity of the dead breaking in on the world of the living. I believe that there are amazing psychological phenomena, not yet brought under the order of any known laws, which may some time be more systematically ordered and controlled. But I should expect, at best, only additions to psychology to come from it, not to theology and certainly not to religion.

But I must confess to a passionate devotion to God as the spiritual reality *par excellence*. If He be real, and if He be concerned for me, I ask no more. I believe that He cares, and that He continues our lives after death in a fellowship of which we have a foretaste here. And I believe that the Eternal Christ, who is this same God, viewed as active and creative, is ever in the world, seeking, knocking, persuading, counseling men to return to their rightful home.

## Prayer

We have been trying to say that the springs and sources of dynamic, creative living lie not in environmental drives and thrusts outside us but deep within us. *Within us* is a meeting place with God, who strengthens and invigorates our whole personality and makes us new creatures, with new values and estimates of the world about us, seen through the eyes of direct and spontaneous love. A leveling of earthly eminences and of earthly obscurities takes place. The tempests and inner strains of self-seeking, self-oriented living grow still. We learn to be worked through; serenity takes the place of anxiety; fretful cares are replaced by a deep and certain assurance. Something of the cosmic patience of God Himself becomes ours, and we walk in quiet assurance and boldness; for He is with us, His rod and His staff they comfort us.

How does one enter upon the internal life of prayer? Dynamic living is not imparted to us by one heavy visitation of God but comes from continuous inner mental habits pursued through years. Inside of us there ought to go on a steady, daily, hourly process of relating ourselves to the Divine Goodness, of opening our lives to His warmth and love, of steadfast surrender to Him, and of sweet whisperings with Him such as we can tell no one about at all. Some of you who read this may be well advanced in this inner practice and able to go far beyond my simple and imperfect experience. Some of you may have seen it from afar; some of you may have lapsed from it after a short time, accepting the secular habits of mind of our secular age, which see only time but not time bathed in eternity and regenerated by eternity.

I do not have in mind those more formal times of private devotion when we turn our backs upon the family and shut the door of our room and read some devotional book and pause in meditation and quiet prayer. Those times are important and need to be cultivated. But the internal prayer life is something still more basic. It is carried on after one has left the quiet room, has opened the door and gone back into the noisy hubbub of the family group. It is carried on as one dashes for a trolley, as one lunches in a cafeteria, as one puts the children to bed. There is a way of living in prayer at the same time that one is busy with the outward affairs of daily living.

This practice of continuous prayer in the presence of God involves developing the habit of carrying on mental life at two levels. At one level we are immersed in this world of time, of daily affairs. At the same time, but at a deeper level of our minds, we are in active relation with the eternal life. I do not think this is a psychological impossibility or an abnormal thing. One sees a mild analogy in the very human experience of being in love. The newly accepted lover has an internal life of joy, of bounding heart, of outgoing aspiration toward his beloved. Yet he goes to work, earns his living, eats his meals, pays his bills. But all the time, deep within, there is a level of awareness of an object very dear to him. This awareness is private; he shows it to no one; yet it spills across and changes his outer life, colors his behavior, and gives new zest and glory to the daily round. Oh yes, we know what a mooning calf he may be at first, what a lovable fool about outward affairs. But when the lover gets things in focus again, and husband and wife settle down to the long pull of the years, the deep love-relation underlies all the raveling frictions of home life and re-creates them in the light of deeper currents. The two levels are there, the surface and the deeper, in fruitful interplay, with the creative values coming from the deeper into the daily affairs of life.

So it is sometimes when one becomes a lover of God. One's first experience of the heavenly splendour plows through one's whole being, makes one dance and sing inwardly, enthralls one in unspeakable love. Then the world, at first, is all out of focus; we scorn it, we are abstracted, we are drunken with eternity. We have not yet learned how to live in both worlds at once, how to integrate our life in time fruitfully with eternity. Yet we are beings whose home is both here and yonder, and we must learn the secret of being at home in both places all the time. A new level of our being has been opened to us, and lo, it is God with us. The experience of the presence of God is not something plastered on to our nature; it is the fulfillment of ourselves. The last deeps of humanity go down into the life of God. The stabilizing of our lives so that we live in God and in time, in fruitful interplay, is the task of maturing religious life.

How do you begin this life at two levels? You begin *now*, wherever you are. Listen to these words outwardly. But within, deep within you, continue in steady prayer, offering yourself and all that you are to Him in simple, joyful, serene, unstrained dedication. Practice it steadily. Make it your conscious intention. Keep it up for days and weeks and years. You will be swept away by rapt attention to the exciting things going on around you. Then catch yourself and bring yourself back. You will forget God for whole hours. But do not waste any time in bitter regrets or self-recriminations. Just begin again. The first weeks and months of such practice are pretty patchy, badly botched. But say inwardly to yourself and to God, "This is the kind of bungling person I am when I am not wholly Thine. But take this imperfect devotion of these months and transmute it with Thy love." Then begin again. And gradually, in months or in three or four years, the habit of heavenly orientation becomes easier, more established. The times of your wandering become shorter, less frequent. The stability of your deeper level becomes greater. God becomes a more steady background of all your reactions in the time-world. Down in this center you have a holy place where you and God hold converse. Your outer behavior will be revised and your personal angularities will be melted down, and you will approach the outer world of men with something more like an outgoing divine love. You begin to love men because you live in love toward God. Or the divine love flows out toward men through you, and you become His pliant instrument of loving concern.

This life is not an introverted life. It is just the opposite of the timid, inturned, self-inspecting life. It is an extravert life. You become turned downward or upward toward God, away from yourself, in joyful self-surrender. You become turned outward toward men in joyful love of them, with new eyes which only love can give; new eyes for suffering, new eyes for hope. Self-consciousness tends to slip away; timidities tend to disappear. You become released from false modesties, for in some degree you have become unimportant, for you have become filled with God. It is amazing how deep humility becomes balanced with boldness, and you become a released, poised, fully normal self. I like a Flemish mystic's name for it, "the established man."

But let us examine more closely this life of inner prayer. First, there is what I can only call *the prayer of oblation*, the prayer of pouring yourself out before God. You pray inwardly, "Take all of me, take all of me." Back behind the scenes of daily occupation you offer yourself steadily to God; you pour out all your life and will and love before Him, and try to keep nothing back. Pour out your triumphs before Him. But pour out also the rags and tatters of your mistakes before Him. If you make a slip and get angry, pour out that bit of anger before Him and say, "That too is Thine." If an evil thought flashes through your mind, pour that out before Him and say, "I know that looks pretty shabby, when it is brought into the sanctuary of Thy holiness. But that's what I am, except Thou aidest me."

When you meet a friend, outwardly you chat with him about trivial things. But inwardly offer him to God. Say within yourself, "Here is my friend. Break in upon him. Melt him down. Help him to shake the scales from his eyes and see Thee. Take him."

Shall I go on and say how far I would carry the prayer of oblation? Some cases may sound strange and silly. Do you stumble on a cinder? Offer it to God as a part of the world that belongs to Him. Do you pass a tree? That too is His; give it to Him as His own. Do you read the newspaper and see the vast panorama of humanity struggling in blindness, in selfish deficient living? Offer humanity in all its shabbiness and in all its grandeur, and hold it up into the heart of Love within you.

At first you make these prayers in words, in little sentences and say them over and over again. "Here is my life, here is my life." In the morning you say, "This is Thy day, this is Thy Day." In the evening you say of the day, "Receive it. Accept it. It is Thine." But in the course of the months you find yourself passing beyond words and living in attitudes of oblation of which the words used to give expression. A gesture of the soul toward God is a prayer; a more or less steady lifting of everything you touch, a lifting of it high before Him to be transmuted in His love. If you grow careless in such unworded gestures and attitudes, you can always return to the practice of worded prayers of oblation to fix your inner attention and retrain your habit of prayer. "Thou wilt keep him in perfect peace whose mind is stayed on Thee."

Then there is the prayer of inward *song*. Phrases run through the background of your mind. "Bless the Lord, O my soul, and all that is within me, bless His holy name." "My soul doth magnify the Lord, and my spirit hath rejoiced in God my Saviour." Inner exultation, inner glorification of the wonders of God fill the deeper level of mind. Sometimes this is a background of deep-running joy and peace; sometimes it is a dancing, singing torrent of happiness, which you must take measures to hide from the world lest men think you are like the apostles at Pentecost, filled with new wine. Pentecost ought to be here; it can be here. Christians who do not know an inner joy are living contradictions of Christianity. Outward sobriety is dictated by a fine sense of the fittingness of things. But inward fires should burn in the God-kindled soul, fires shining outward in a radiant and released personality. Inwardly, there are hours of joy in God, and the songs of the soul are ever rising. Sometimes the singer and the song seem to be merged together as a single offering to the God of joy. Sometimes He who puts the new song into our mouths seems merged with the song and the singer, and it is not we alone who sing, but the eternal lover who sings through us and out into the world where songs have died on many lips.

In such moods I find the Book of Psalms wonderfully helpful. There we come into contact with souls who have risen above debate and argument and problem-discussion, and have become singers of the song of eternal love. We read the Psalms hungrily. They say in words what we try to express. Our private joy in God becomes changed into a fellowship of singing souls. The writers of the Psalms teach us new songs of the heart. They give us great phrases that go rolling through our minds all the day long. They channel our prayer of song. Religious reading ought not to be confined to heady, brainy, argumentative discussion, important as that is. Every profoundly religious soul ought to rise to the level of inward singing; he ought to read devotional literature that is psalmlike in character and spirit. The little book of prayers, *A Chain of Prayers across the Ages,* is excellent. And Thomas à Kempis' *Imitation of Christ* often gives voice to the song of the soul.

Then there is the prayer of inward listening. Perhaps this is not a separate type of prayer, but an element that interlaces the whole of the internal prayer-life. For prayer is a two-way process. It is not just human souls whispering to God. It passes over into communion, with God active in us as well as we active toward God. A specific state of expectancy, of openness of soul is laid bare and receptive before the Eternal Goodness. In quietness we wait, inwardly, in unformulated expectation. Perhaps this is best done in retirement. Our church services ought to be times when bands of expectant souls gather and wait before Him. But too often, for myself, the external show of the ritual keeps my expectations chained to earth, to this room, to see what the choir will sing, to hear how the minister handles his theme. Much of Protestant worship seems to me to keep expectation at the earthly level of watchfulness for helpful external stimuli, external words, external suggestions. Perhaps because I am a Quaker I find the prayer of expectation and of listening easiest to carry on in the silence of solitary and of group meditation.

Creative, spirit-filled lives do not arise until God is attended to, until His internal teaching in warm immediacy becomes a real experience. He has many things to say to us, but we cannot hear Him now because we have not been wholly weaned away from outward helps, valuable as these often are. The living Christ teaches the listening soul and guides him into new truth. Sad is it if our church program is so filled with noise, even beautiful sound, that it distracts us from the listening life, the expectation directed toward God. A living silence is often more creative, more recreative, than verbalized prayers worded in gracious phrases.

We need also times of silent waiting alone when the busy intellect is not leaping from problem to problem and from puzzle to puzzle. If we learn the secret of carrying a living silence in the center of our being we can listen on the run. The listening silence can become intertwined with all our inward prayers. A few moments of relaxed silence alone every day are desperately important. When distracting noises come, do not fight against them; do not elbow them out, but accept them and weave them into the silence. Does the wind rattle the window? Then pray, "So let the wind of the Spirit shake the Christian church into life." Does a child cry in the street outside? Then pray, "So cries my infant soul, which does not know the breadth of Thy heart."

The last reaches of religious education are not attained by carefully planned and externally applied lessons, taught to people through the outward ears. The fundamental religious education of the soul is conducted by the Holy Spirit, the living voice of God within us. He is the last and greatest teacher of the soul. All else is but pointings to the inward teacher, the Spirit of the indwelling Christ. Until life is lived in the presence of this teacher, we are apt to confuse knowledge of church history and Biblical backgrounds with the true education of the soul that takes place in the listening life of prayer.

A fourth form of inner prayer is what I call the prayer of *carrying*. This I shall not try to develop now, but shall discuss later in connection with the experience of group fellowship among those who are deep in the life and love of God. But it consists essentially in a well-nigh continuous support of some particular souls who are near to you in the things of the inner life.

I must, however, speak more at length of a fifth aspect of internal prayer. The Catholic books call it *infused* prayer. There come times, to some people at least, when one's prayer is given to one as it were from beyond oneself. Most of the time we ourselves seem to pick the theme of our prayer. We seem to be the conscious initiators. But there come amazing times in the practice of prayer when our theme of prayer is laid upon us as if initiated by God himself. This is an astonishing experience. It is as if we were being prayed through by a living Spirit. How can it be that the indwelling Christ prompts us to breathe back to God a prayer that originates in Himself? Is there a giant circle such that prayer may originate in God and swing down into us and back up unto Himself? I can only say that it seems to be that way. And it seems to be an instance of the giant circle in religious dedication, whereby we seek because we have already been found by Him. Our seeking is already His finding. Our return to the Father is but the completion of His going out to us.

In the experience of infused prayer there seems to be some blurring of the distinctions between the one who prays, the prayer that is prayed, and the One to whom the prayer is prayed. Do *we* pray, or does God pray through us? I know not. All I can say is that prayer is taking place, and that we are graciously permitted to be within the orbit. We emerge from such experiences of infused prayer shaken and deepened and humbled. And we somehow know that we have been given some glimpse of that life, that center of wonder before Whom every knee should bow and every tongue that knows the language of its homeland should confess the adorable mercy of God.

I have tried, in these words, to keep very close to the spirit and practice of my three dearest spiritual friends and patterns, outside of Jesus of Nazareth. They are Brother Lawrence and St. Francis of Assisi and John Woolman. Of these, Brother Lawrence, who lived in Lorraine three hundred years ago, is the simplest. He spent his life in the practice of the presence of God, and a priceless little book of counsels, by that name, has come down to us. John Woolman, a New Jersey Quaker of two hundred years ago, really so ordered his external life as to attend above all to the inner teacher and never lose touch with Him. But greatest of all is Francis of Assisi, whose direct and simple and joyous dedication of soul led him close to men and to God till he reproduced in amazing degree the life of Jesus. It is said of St. Francis not merely that he prayed, but that he became a prayer. Such lives must be reborn today if the life of the eternal love is to break through the heavy encrustations of our conventional church life, and apostolic life and love and power can be restored to the church of God. He can break through any time we are really willing.

### Fellowship

When our souls are utterly swept through and overturned by God's invading love, we suddenly find ourselves in the midst of a wholly new relationship with some of our fellow men. We find ourselves enmeshed with some people in amazing bonds of love and nearness and togetherness of soul, such as we never knew before. In glad amazement we ask ourselves: What is this startling new bondedness in love which I feel with those who are down in the same center of life? Can this amazing experience of togetherness in love be what men have called fellowship? Can this be the love which bound together the early church, and made their meals together into a sacrament of love? Is this internal impulse which I feel, to share life with those who are down in the same center of love, the reason that the early church members shared their outward goods as a symbol of the experienced internal sharing of the life and the love of Christ? Can this new bondedness in love be the meaning of being in the Kingdom of God?

But not all our acquaintances are caught within these new and special bonds of love. A rearrangement takes place. Some people whom we had only slightly known before suddenly become electrically illuminated. Now we know them, for lo, they have been down in the center a long time, and we never knew their secret before. Now we are bound together with them in a special bond of nearness, far exceeding the nearness we feel toward many we have known for years. For we know where they live, and they know where we live, and we understand one another and are powerfully drawn to one another. We hunger for their fellowship; their lives are knitted with our life in this amazing bondedness of divine love.

Others of our acquaintance recede in importance. We may have known them for years, we may have thought we were close together. But now we know they are not down in the center in Christ, where our dearest loves and hopes of life and death are focused. And we know we can never share life at its depth until they, too, find their way down into this burning center of shared love.

Especially does a new alignment of our church relationship take place. Now we know from within the secret of the perseverance and fidelity of some, a secret we could not have guessed when we were *outside* them. *Now* we see suddenly that some of the active leaders are not so far down into the center of peace and love as we had supposed. We had always respected and admired them for their energy, but now we know they have never been brought into the depths, nor do they know the secret of being rooted and grounded with others in love. Now we suddenly see that some quiet obscure persons, whose voices count for little in the councils of the church, are princes and saints in Israel. Why had we not noticed them before? The whole graded scale by which we had arranged the people in our church according to importance is shaken and revised. Some of the leaders are greater even than we had guessed; others are thin and anxious souls, not knowing the peace at the center. Some that stood low are really high in the new range of values.

Into this fellowship of souls at the center we simply emerge. No one is chosen to the fellowship. When we discover God we discover the fellowship. When we find ourselves in Christ we find we are also amazingly united with those others who are also in Christ. When we were outside of it we never knew that it existed or only dimly guessed the existence of bonds of love among those who were dedicated slaves of Christ. There are many who are members of our churches who do not know what I am speaking of. But there are others of you who will say, "Surely I know exactly what you are talking about. I'm glad you've found your way in."

But, sad to say, there are many who know the word "fellowship" but think it applies only to church sociability. Such people organize church suppers and call them fellowship suppers. What a horrible prostitution of a sacred bond! Our church suppers and church programs which aim at mere sociability are not down at the bottom. You can't build a church that is Christ's church on mere sociability, important and normal as that is. Churches that are rooted and grounded in Christ are built upon this inner amazing fellowship of souls who know a shared devotion to God.

If fellowship in this rich, warm sense has vanished from a church, there may be enough endowments to keep the institution going, but the life is gone. Churches can go on for years on endowment incomes and tributes levied upon personal pride. But they are only sounding brass or tinkling cymbals if group interknittedness in the joyous bonds of Christ is gone. Where the bondedness of souls in a common enslavement is present, though you meet in a barn, you have a church.

In the fellowship barriers are surprisingly leveled. Cultural differences do not count in the love of God. Educational differences do not count. The carpenter and the banker exchange experiences in their practice of communion with God, and each listens respectfully, attentively to the other. For God in His inner working does not respect these class lines which we so carefully erect. In real fellowship, theological differences are forgotten, and liberals and conservatives eagerly exchange experiences concerning the wonders of the life of devotion.

Most of us are reticent about speaking our deepest thoughts, or exposing our inner tenderness to public gaze. And much of this reticence is right. But there ought to be some times when, and there ought to be some people with whom we open up our hearts on the deep things of the spirit. Normal religious development cannot take place in a vacuum occupied solely by you and God. We need friends of the soul. Fellowship is not an accidental addition to religion. It is the matrix within which we bear one another's aspirations. Do you have people with whom you feel it right to open your heart? If you have not, if you are stilted and stiff and embarrassed, and have no one to whom to confess, not your sins, but your joys, you are indeed an unfortunate soul. George Fox has counsel which I prize very much: "Know one another in that which is eternal." Churches ought to be places where men may know one another *in that which is eternal*. But in many a church the gulf between individuals on the deep things of God is an impassable gulf, and souls are starving and dying of inner loneliness. Would that we could break through our crust of stilted, conventional reserve, and make our churches centers of a living communion of the saints.

The last depths of conversation in the fellowship go beyond spoken words. People who know one another in God do not need to talk much. They know one another already. In the last depths of understanding, words cease and we sit in silence together yet in perfect touch with one another, more bound into the common life by the silence than we ever were by words.

Some time ago I was in Germany, visiting isolated Friends throughout that country. One man I met was a factory worker. He spoke ungrammatical German. His teeth were discolored, his shoulders were stooped. He spoke the Swabian dialect. But he was a radiant soul, a quiet, reticent saint of God. He knew the inner secrets of the life that is clothed in God. We were drawn together by invisible currents. We knew each other immediately, more deeply than if we had been neighbors for twenty years. I called at his simple home near Stuttgart. He motioned me to escape from the rest of the visitors and come into the bedroom. There, leaning on the window sills, we talked together. Immediately we gravitated to the wonders of prayer and of God's dealing with the soul. I told him of some new insights that had recently come to me. He listened and nodded confirmation, for he already knew those secrets. He understood and could tell me of things of the Spirit of which I had only begun to guess. I feel sure that I knew more history and mathematics and literature and philosophy than did he. And the social gulf in Germany between a professor and a factory man is infinitely wide. But that afternoon I was taught by him and nourished by him, and we looked at each other eye to eye and knew a common love of Christ. Then as the afternoon shadows fell and dissolved with twilight, our words became less frequent, until they ceased altogether. And we mingled our lives in the silence, for we needed no words to convey our thoughts. I have only had one letter from him in the year, but we are as near to each other now, every day, as we were that afternoon.

And now I must speak of the internal prayer of carrying, which I mentioned above. Within the fellowship there is an experience of relatedness with one another, a relation of upholding one another by internal bonds of prayer that I can only call the prayer of carrying. Between those of the fellowship there is not merely a sense of unity when we are together physically; with some this awareness of being bonded through a common life continues almost as vividly when separated as when together. This awareness of our life as in their lives and their lives as in our life is a strange experience. It is as if the barriers of individuality were let down, and we shared a common life and love. A subterranean, internal relation of supporting those who are near to us in the fellowship takes place. We know that they, too, hold us up by the strength of their bondedness. Have you had the experience of being carried and upheld and supported? I do not mean the sense that God is upholding you alone. It is the sense that some people you know are lifting you and offering you and upholding you in your inner life. And do you carry some small group of acquaintances toward whom you feel a peculiar nearness, people who rest upon your hearts not as obligations but as fellow travelers? Through the day you quietly hold them high before God in inward prayer, giving them to Him, vicariously offering your life and strength to become their life and strength.

This is very different from conventional prayer lists. These are not a chance group of people. They are your special burden and your special privilege. No two people have the same group to whom they are bound in this special nearness. Each person is the center of radiating bonds of spiritual togetherness. If everyone who names the name of Jesus were faithful in this inner spiritual obligation of carrying, the intersections would form a network of bondedness whereby the members of the whole living church would be carrying one another in outgoing bonds of love and prayer and support.

At the time of the ceremony of the sacrament of Communion, this bondedness is experienced; separate selves are swept together and welded into one life. There is a way of continuing this communion through daily life. No outward bread and wine need be present, but inwardly we feed with our fellows from the Holy Grail and meet one another in spirit. This mystical unity, this group togetherness of soul, lies at the heart of the living church.

I have tried to emphasize the Inner Teacher. In us all is a life upspringing. It is the Holy Spirit. He speaks within. He teaches us things we can never learn in books. He makes vivid and dynamic what were formerly dead phrases. He integrates us and leads us into new truths. He lays on us new burdens. He sensitizes us in new areas, toward God and toward men.

# 2

# CHRIST IN CATASTROPHE

*And then Christ himself was in my cell in prison, saying,*
*"Blessed are the poor in spirit. . . . Blessed are the meek. . . .*
*Blessed are the peacemakers. . . ." I heard the question, "Is*
*that true?" And I was able to say in great joy and peace, "It*
*is true."*

EMIL FUCHS

Emil Fuchs is a German Quaker who found serenity of spirit through great suffering in Nazi Germany. A teacher of religion and a member of the Religious Socialists, he was dismissed from his college and imprisoned when Hitler came to power. Released, he was able to assist the escape of refugees by operating a car hire business and later to travel about Germany lecturing to small groups. Great difficulties visited his family: flight, illness of body and mind, death. Out of these Emil Fuchs emerged with the smile of the child, the saint who can bear the hardness of the world without losing his own softness of spirit. In 1949, at the age of 75, he accepted the post of Professor of Religion at the University of Leipzig so that he might put again before his countrymen the challenge which he puts in *Christ in Catastrophe,* an inward record written in 1949.

One terrible, bitter question torments us when we see the mighty success of what we believe is wrong, when we see that millions of persons, hundreds even of our friends, go along with this success. It is the question: "Are you alone right and all others wrong?" Are you mad or are they? Are those right who tell us that in this sinful world a politician must go the way of cleverness and deceit, fraud and violence?

Even my friends put this question to me when success

after success came to Hitler. Yearly his power grew. More and more it became dangerous to speak aloud for freedom and peace and reconciliation. You could never know when a meeting would be raided by Storm Troopers and the audience and speakers misused, even killed. More and more we became lonely people. Many persons—leaders of churches, professors, teachers, pastors—became silent or went over to Hitler, not daring to show friendship to those who went on speaking against him. Friends warned us. The President of our Academy in Kiel said to me, "Please be silent. Do not give public lectures any more. Then perhaps we can save you."

In March 1933 Hitler came to power. In three months some hundred thousands of persons were killed, taken into concentration camps, or forced to flee. Many who had stood firm until then succumbed before a danger they had never imagined.

I was dismissed from my professorship in Kiel and imprisoned. My youngest son hid himself because he had been sentenced to be lynched by the students at Kiel, where he had been a leader of anti-Nazis. My eldest son and daughter were in great danger. A high official of the Ministry of Education in Berlin tried to build a golden bridge for me, asking if I would not try to instruct myself better about National Socialism and show hope of joining. I answered that I was quite clear; it would be absolutely impossible for me to be connected with the movement.

People who fell into Nazi hands were treated with cruelty, and I was in great anxiety. One night I became nearly mad. I saw my children, cruelly killed, lying before me. And in this hour of utter despair I heard a voice saying, "What do you want? Shall they save their lives by losing their conscience?" I was able to say, "They shall keep their conscience."

Peace came to me. From that moment I could bear the hardships my children had to go through.

And then Christ himself was in my cell in prison, saying, "Blessed are the poor in spirit. . . . Blessed are they that mourn. . . . Blessed are the meek. . . . Blessed are they which do hunger and thirst after righteousness. . . . Blessed are the pure in heart. . . . Blessed are the peacemakers. . . ." I heard the question, "Is that true?" And I was able to say in great joy and peace, "It is true."

During the continuing hours of anxiety and fear, it was my only help that the presence of the living Christ was with me. I remember many meetings in silence with friends and many lonely hours in which a Divine Presence strengthened us and gave freshness and insight. Then there came an hour of deepest need. My eldest daughter, worn out by what she had endured for her convictions, died a very bitter death, and in the hour of her burial I went into the chapel in utter darkness of spirit. But there the presence of God surged around us. It was so strong that all felt him, even one man, irreligious and a national socialist, who said to me, "What is this? In this hour I feel such a power as I have never before felt in my life."

*Was It Human Imagination?*

That I saw him, that I heard his voice, that might have been imagination. But what cannot be imagination is the new life, the strength and the insight which his presence gave. No mere imagination, no impact out of the subconscious mind can give a father the strength to face danger to his children and remain certain and full of peace because they go the way of their conscience. No imagination can overcome the darkness in which you live when a person you love is handled with cruelty and forced into fits of fear and despair of mind. You are hopeless; you must look on while mind and life are destroyed by suffering. Nothing which is of imagination only can bring out of that revulsion peace: the overpowering awareness of an eternal love whose ways you do not undestand, whose will you have to accept without comprehension, but whose reality you know.

I know that I experienced in terrible hours the reality that the disciples experienced in the resurrection, that Paul experienced on the road to Damascus. They saw and heard him. That may have been imagination, vision, hallucination. But his being, his reality touched them and became a new strength in them. So strong was this reality that they could cry out his message, not only without the fear that had hindered them, but also with a power that told other people of the same reality.

I think that we who have to go through terrible times of great catastrophe in the changing world have also this grace from God, that once again he makes it possible for us to see his reality clearly, more clearly than the generations before us. The word of the Epistle of John is again true: "That which was from the beginning, which we have heard, which we have seen . . . declare we unto you."

With assurance and unshakeable peace in Christ's presence, I began in prison to set down an account of the New Testament, beginning with the *Gospel of Matthew* and the *Sermon on the Mount*. I wrote of Christ's gospel and of seeing in it our own sufferings. There were difficulties and dangers, searchings and warnings, but it was possible to send this writing out. And it was possible in later jouurneys to bring it to friends. That Christ had given me a new work to do, a new opportunity to carry his message seemed to me then and seems to me now like another miracle. Before this it had seemed as if the ordinances of Hitler and the power of the secret police made impossible every work for peace and the message of Christ.

Was it imagination that enabled people like me to know, from the beginning of all the propaganda, that the spirit of Hitler was not of God? Why did so very many, very clever and orthodox theological thinkers, scholars, pastors and leaders of churches not recognize evil? Many churchmen and church people, liberal and orthodox, went with evil until evil went against them. Without their help Hitler would have been impossible. But they were worshippers of nation and lovers of armies first, and afterwards Christians. They had Christianity as doctrine, very elaborate, very refined, very traditional; but they had not that experience in which the living Christ, the risen Lord, gives his call and task for this day and this time—out of the same spirit in which he taught his disciples two thousand years ago.

## Two Thousand Years Ago and Today

It is the great mystery of the history of men that the Eternally Creative speaks to us in the humble poor carpenter of Nazareth. We do not know very much of him. If we read the Gospels, which are only the reflection of him in the minds of unlettered people, his sentences look simple. It is as if a child had formed them. But then some of them begin to speak to our mind, to our condition, and they challenge our inward being. And in challenging us they begin to lay a task upon us: to be perfect "even as your Father which is in heaven is perfect." "Your Father?" How that unfathomable mystery holds out a goal for us poor finite beings. More and more its challenging power becomes a changing power in our lives, and we begin to experience, to live some part of the creative mystery itself.

Then we read the story of his suffering and death on the cross. Helpless he is. He does not ask his followers to defend him, so they lose confidence in him and in his cause. He does not try to flee or to avoid the traps of his enemies by clever devices, and he does not deny the message which is bringing him to death. Helpless he dies, only knowing that he goes the way of him who called him, whose purpose, whose will he accepts even though not understanding them.

It is really a very bewildering story. But again it begins to speak to our condition and again it challenges. We begin to realize that here a very simple man, this carpenter of Nazareth, challenges the authorities of this world, this so-ciety—his time, our time—those priests and scribes, these preachers and scholars, those Caesars, these Hitlers with all their faith in soldiers and weapons, devices and money and all that is used to oppress. He challenges us, poor finite per-sons that we are, that we may be men, perfect, pure in heart, hungry for goodness, yearning for peace, denying of violence, and thus victorious throughout the earth. And the goal is shown to us not only for individuals but for mankind. There shall be a uniting power and changing love, by which we will be led to create the society of the meek, who are stronger than the strong; the society of the loving, who cannot be broken by force; the society of those who live in the truth that rends the power of insincerity. The kingdom of God shall be built by those who can suffer and forgive and love, and overcome evil with good.

The disciples had fled. They were wholly discouraged by his strange inactiveness before the might of his enemies. And then we do not know exactly what happened. We have different stories and they do not give us one clear picture. Most of them seem to come from the experience of later times. But still we know that the challenge was again in the disciples' minds, that their innermost beings were roused and changed by it. They were quite certain that he again stood beside them and that his word and being met them. So mighty was the challenge that they saw him and heard his words. Visions and hallucinations? Yes. But breaking forth out of them was the live experience of the power that touched and changed their inward being. They became messengers, writing down as well as they could what manner of challenge had come into them.

And so it is now. In every generation, the challenge comes to those who struggle to grasp a meaning of life, even amid the ugly, greedy, acquisitive world around them. Behold today pathetic men driven on by stupid passions of greed and power to spoil their own inner purity and that of others around them. But behold, also, the fresh challenge of the carpenter who lived in the creative power of God and who died against the spirit of this world. So people are always experiencing anew the resurrection; so faith renews itself through the centuries, not through belief in outward miracles—no tale of old miracles can give you faith—but through the inward experience of a power living today.

Thus the reality of his resurrection broke into my life. It broke in as a clear, strong security in the hardest hour of trial and suffering and made me strong, gave me peace, and made me able to work and speak in joy.

He stood before me. He stands before mankind, asking us all, asking the nations and the leaders of nations, the statesmen and the simple people, whether they will destroy themselves or whether they will give themselves to the grip of his power and find thereby a new life in which love, not greed or lust for power, is the new dynamic.

*The Iron Yoke*

In the summer of 1947 I spent six weeks in Switzerland visiting my son whom I had not seen for twelve years. It was the first time I had been outside bewildered Germany since 1932. Then I returned home with a new eye for everything. When I travelled on the crowded trains or streetcars, I saw with a new sharpness the expressions on the faces around me. I see them now: the offended faces, saying, "How can such hard things happen to me, a respectable law-abiding person?" The hard faces, saying, "I will win again what I have lost. I have no time to care for others." Then there are the empty faces, the unfulfilled eyes of this man or this woman, who goes on doing his daily task and earning his living, no longer seeing meaning or hope. There are blank faces, too, behind which stand evil secrets, things that a man hides from himself while still he finds no rest. There are faces which say, "I will be happy and forget." These faces I see more and more as things improve and as more and more people try to begin a happy life of forget-fulness of past suffering, past despair. But where is there strength, where real life in forgetting?

I see these faces now, and sometimes among them I see a face on which it is written that this man, this woman over-came suffering and despair, that behind the face is serenity, a conscience at rest and yet awake to love, truth, helpfulness.

But when I see all the faces, I suspect that many of them, particularly in Germany but perhaps in other places, say, "I am offended." I long and pray to give them this one thing: that they may be able to accept their fate, accept their suffering—not trying to flee, to evade, to forget, to hide it from themselves—simply to accept.

Millions suffer terribly. Millions had to die, had to give sons and daughters, their hope for life and future. Is one per-son alone to be spared? Can he wish to be spared? To the empty eyes, I would say, "Look around. Quite near is a man a woman, a child, a human being suffering as you suffer; try to be a comrade to them, help if you can help and, if you cannot, be full of that sympathy that gives strength. See, in so doing you will overcome helplessness and emptiness and a new meaning will come to you. For in that helpful love you will experience the changing power of the eternal God."

And to those out of whose eyes speak hidden fears and

secrets, I would say, "Accept, accept and look at what you have done in an evil hour. Accept it and take the challenge of him who calls to a new life and a deep changing of heart." I say it again because it cannot be said too often, "Accept your fate, your suffering, accept it as a call out of the power of God, who challenges both in happiness and suffering, challenges us to overcome evil and suffering in truth and love."

To those of my own nation who try to forget, I would say, "We have not the right to forget the disaster to which we brought the whole world and to which we brought ourselves. Forgetting means that we do not overcome ambition, servility, love of arms; the tragic background of so much in our nation, the tragic block to the great possibilities we still possess." We are in the situation of Jeremiah, who said to his nation, "Thus saith the Lord; Thou hast broken the yoke of wood; but thou shalt make for them yokes of iron." We have to bear the iron yoke and we have to bear it with our nation. I take that part, forgiving those of my own people who made it so hard, and forgiving also those of other lands who made it harder than it need have been. That man has no need to forget who knows what forgiveness is. Through it something of the redeeming power of the cross comes into his life. Out of suffering and scarcity we create fellowship and peace and happiness for our children and grandchildren.

You, what will you do? Live on in selfishness, forgetting the experiences of the war, shifting the burden from your shoulders to the shoulders of others, creating antagonism, hatred, strife, war again and again? Or will you take your yoke on your own shoulder, not asking whether you—or others—made it heavy, and change it to a cross?

## Despair

The winter of 1941 was very cold. Hitler was at the height of his power; France was conquered, victorious German armies were fighting in Russia. Two young men came to me. They had sometimes attended our meeting for worship. More I did not know of them. They asked me whether I could come with them. They brought me to a large dining room of a private house where a score or more of young people were assembled, some officers, some soldiers, some civilians, some women, too. One of them said, "All of us have been enthusiastic followers of Hitler. We volunteered for the army. Now we have just had leave and we have to return to our different places in the army. This is our last meeting together, and we do not know whether we shall see each other again. But during these days at home we have all realized that we no longer have faith in Hitler. We see that his whole propaganda is a lie to hold him and his party in power. And now we have no hope. Can you say something to us that will give us hope?"

It could have been a trap of the secret police, but it was necessary to speak.

They had been roused by clever passionate propaganda to a blind fanaticism for which the "nation" was the last ideal, the only value in the world worth dying for. They had been taught, and they had accepted, that it was right to lie for the nation, to deceive, to trick, to kill. Then, slowly and terribly the suspicion had risen that this last ideal might itself be an untruth, a means of deceit—a lie fostered to support the power and egotism of men who lived in might and splendor while others went out to die.

Helpless and empty, these young people were going out to fight, perhaps to die. What could I tell them?

"For outward greatness and happiness, I can not give you any hope or faith," I began. "We are rushing to a catastrophe for our nation greater than we can imagine."

Then I told them of a letter from a refugee, who wrote out of very hard experiences, "We had not thought that our way would be so hard. But if we had to choose again, we would choose the same way."

"What a difference," I said. "Hitler and your cause in splendid success and you lose faith and hope. And here a refugee, in distress, writing, 'We would choose the same way again.' For this man and his conscience the nation is not the highest measure. He knows about man and the value of a man. He knows of a world of truth and justice which is higher than man, and which a man can realize in his work, and, by his work, in mankind. He obeyed a call. So in his distress he has hope and faith.

"In your very despair, this call is here for you today. You will have to go through more hard experiences. If you come back from the war, you will find a broken-down country: like you, full of hopelessness and misery. Then the question will be whether there is a higher strength in your life. Do you belong to those who in their egotism lament their misery and poverty and seek to find a way out only for themselves? Or do you belong to those who see a way of help for others, who see that outward power and armies are unnecessary to great things? If you do, you will have a great work to do, and your life will have strength and meaning.

"It may be that some will not come back, that some have to die in war. If they have only despair and hopelessness, their life is lost in a lost cause. But if they are able to hear the message of hope and give it on to a single friend in his own despair, then life is in them and works on after them, a part of that eternal life which can never be extinguished.

"In Jesus the faith in success to which millions succumb is challenged. This world, which seeks salvation and life in selfishness, in cleverness, in power and money, splendor and pride—this world is challenged.

" 'The meek . . . shall inherit the earth.' "

*Can There Be Happiness?*

When I live through beautiful spring days or a summer such as we had this year, or when I have opportunity to live in a happy family with children, I often think of the young mother who lost her child one winter, and when spring came, cried out bitterly, "My child cannot see it."

There are millions in this world today in whom this cry lives, millions for whom the beauty of nature in the spring and all the happiness of other people are only terrible pains, making despair harder to bear. Have we any right to enjoy anything, to be happy with our families when we know of the millions in despair?

I not only say that we can enjoy; I say that we must find again the strength to enjoy—but not by forgetting what we have lost or what others have lost, certainly not by forgetting our shortcomings and our sins. There is another, stronger way.

There was a time when beauty and happiness only deepened my own despair and pain. The spring and summer of 1933 were good to look upon. But my children were scattered, my family destroyed, my life's work broken. My friends were in danger; some had fled; others had been imprisoned; many had been killed. And around me was the success of what I knew was the power of destruction and injustice. I hated the beauty of that spring and I fled the sight of families and the sounds of music. Hiding its terrors behind sparkling life made fate seem doubly cruel.

But then came the experience of Christ's presence, and it became stronger and stronger in my being. And out of it came again the challenge of him who was happy with children, who calls us to enjoy the lilies of the field and the birds of the air. More and more it came to me that all joy and happiness are great gifts of God, his greetings, showing us some-

thing of the goal which will be achieved when love and truth
are victorious on earth. In the beauty of nature, in the lively
innocence of children, in the joys and pleasures of young
people, I felt more and more a hidden presence. All joy is
holy.

Because he violates what should be holy, man brings suffering into this world. He loses and then destroys the reverence owed to all life, all happiness, all real joy. Can we not
save these for ourselves so that our suffering will be a means
of saving them for others? Only now perhaps we know what
joy really is, only now, taught by bitter suffering, when we
see the deep holiness of all life. Even when we do not have
joy for ourselves, we can reverence it in others.

Do not, therefore, close your eyes before the sufferings of
your neighbors. Do not fear that it will destroy your happiness if you live in sympathy with them. This indeed brings
something like a shadow into your life, and at the first moment you feel you cannot endure it; so you try to forget it.
No. Hold it fast; take it into your life. Bring it into touch
with your own happiness and joy. All that is only superficial
will vanish, but the real happiness of family, of art and song,
of nature and friendship and devotion—all will grow and
become more real until they become that holiness in which
they are a part of God's presence in our lives.

### Love's Great Help

My daughter had died. Her husband was a refugee. We
did not know where he was. All my other children were scattered through the world. I was alone with the boy of four
years who had lost his mother. It was a time of helpless darkness out of which only the miracle of which I have told
could have saved me. Life was so full of pain that every
happiness seemed sin. But what would become of the boy?
Must I not live for him? And if I lived for him, should I

be a sad empty-hearted grandfather, never happy and never bringing happiness? Oh, I knew that a child will not talk, will not even sit beside you if he does not find happiness. But God gave me love for this boy, and I could be happy with him, more and more happy, and through him alive to the joy of other people.

Is not failure to enjoy other people's happiness a very real source of hatred and unrest? There is envy, because you feel the success of other people's work or the handsomeness of their children or the peace of their home—or even the helpful spirit by which they try to make you happy. An important truth: if we can share other people's joys and happiness, we find an important link uniting us with them. If we cannot, we will be separated from them—even if we do mighty works to help them in their need.

It is a great thing to help others, to comfort them in sadness and to strengthen them in deep suffering. I often say to a person who cannot overcome his suffering: try to find a person to whom you can bring help and strength in his life. Christ's love then will greet you and strengthen you. But the same is true, perhaps more true, of sharing joy. It is possible only if the joy of others is your joy. How good is the experience of man in deep suffering, when, look, he sees before him the chance to bring a small bit of joy to a child.

When people have to go through really deep sorrow, when something of the fundamentals of their lives is destroyed, they feel as if they walk and live under a great glass bowl. They see and hear other people, but they seem separated from them by an intense pain that others, even the most sympathetic, cannot feel. But if love works its great miracle, it reaches through the invisible wall. You do not forget what you lost, but sometimes you think that now for the first time you feel the innermost reality and beauty of joy, the creative power which comes to you out of it.

Thus to men and women struggling amid the hard sorrows of life, there is given something of the charm which Jesus means when he says, "Become as little children." It is the secret of serene old men and women who have come through a life full of sorrow and hard work, and who perhaps have to go on in more pain and more toil. Suffering and joy are in a miraculous way connected with each other in this world of God.

## Can These Things Be?

How desperately people ask, "How can God be love, when all still happens that has happened in the world of men— and will go on happening in time to come?"

The same world with the same history cries out to me in a clear voice, "God is love."

If God is love and you hate your brother, you live without God. You live without the one creative power of life. Do you wonder that you live in a world of death? Three or four thousand years ago, a poet said:

> Thou sendest forth thy spirit; they are created.
> Thou hidest thy face, they are troubled.
> Thou takest away thy breath, they die,
> And return to their dust.

When men and whole generations of men and whole nations and civilizations seek their life from wealth and power and oppression and injustice, when they live without love in greed and hate, they separate themselves from God and return to their dust.

When nations and civilizations have to die, as in the times we live in, a stream of death and terror runs over the earth. It is not because God is far away, but because man in his hatred and selfishness does not reach out to him, does not reach out to the creative power around him, even within him. God asks more from us than to be small, narrow, selfish, respectable people going the way of money-getting and traditional righteousness. He asks us to be strong upright people who dare to give happiness and life for him and for his kingdom. He created man out of the animals by making him hear this call, and as long as we hear it, so long do we live as men, and his strength is in us. When we do not hear this call, we are living in nothing better than narrow selfishness. Great achievements and discoveries become mere instruments of this selfishness. Hatred and antagonism grow. Man and his civilization begin to die in all the torments of death.

God's love is in this, that he gave us a great goal. The challenge of God's love may therefore be a terror for man. We have to decide whether we pass through this terror into peace and certainty of life's meaningfulness or whether we shrink from it into destruction. Just as those who crucified Christ had to decide, so we also have to decide: whether we shall hear his challenge and seek the way of truth, love and brotherhood, or whether we will again crucify him in all his suffering brothers and sisters—and return to our dust.

### Christ Recrucified

Some times we wonder why in the books, letters and testimonies of Jesus' time and immediately after, there is no mention of him. For the great men of Rome and Greece the happenings in Galilee and Jerusalem were as the news of the lynching of a Negro in an unknown township of the South is to people nowadays. They read, shudder a little and forget. And if a destitute Negro is lynched, or if a hungry child dies in China, or if a drunken man stumbles through the slums of Philadelphia, or if a rich man supports a Hitler or otherwise oppresses freedom and truth, sacrificing righteousness to profits, then in each of these events is Christ's challenge: How much of God may there have been in this your brother, your sister, whom you killed, starved, denied education and constructive living, or drowned in luxury?

"Inasmuch as ye have done it unto one of the least of these my brethren, ye have done it unto me. . . . Inasmuch as ye did it not to one of the least of these, ye did it not to me."

There are many in whom Christ's challenge mingles in a strange way with the traditional, inherited faith in force. Such people try to help their suffering brothers by fighting against those who oppress them. And there are other ways of trying to join obedience to Christ with obedience to tradition. There are the churches which try to speak his message clearly, and yet tremble to offend the easygoing, the comfortable and the influential. There are the millions of men who mingle the challenge they hear with an egoistic longing for a more comfortable life and for materialistic striving. But at the same time there is the growing number of those, very often trembling like the disciples, who are forced by a divine challenge to stand and struggle and work and speak, bringing people to a clear understanding of Christ's way and to a clear decision between him and tradition, injustice, self-deceit and force.

We must know, all of us, that we are fighting against him insofar as we hinder any of our brothers from finding his own constructive life. And we know that we stand for him —again, all of us—insofar as we stand for the rights of others, for understanding and peace and truth and justice, and—most important of all—insofar as we are prepared to sacrifice our comfort and our privilege for the lives and rights of our brothers.

## Experience and Authority

Again and again men have tried to tell us various things about God: how he is and what he is and how he created the world and how Jesus became his revelation. Men have put together their accounts out of the Bible or out of their heads, and again and again we have to recognize that God is too great a mystery for us to comprehend. He is dwelling in the Light unto which no man can approach. The creative mystery of the world cannot be known through man-made doctrines and teachings. God put in the midst of history a simple man, pure in heart and strong in truth, giving in him the message of what we shall be and what mankind will be.

And behind this man stands the history by which God taught a nation to come to an understanding of a great goal roused in the inward being of its prophets and leaders. In this history the Bible tells us of Abraham, who had to go out from his father's house in a higher search; of Moses, who had to take the shoes from off his feet; of Isaiah, who saw God in the Temple; of Ezekiel, who saw him by the river Chebar; of all the prophets and poets, who denounced unrighteousness and sang redemption.

What all these men saw of God and can tell of him is the image of the eternal mystery in the human mind. We know that they experienced his challenge to them and his call to their people; we know that the continuing reality of his self-revealing leads to Jesus.

So we read the Bible, not to construct doctrines about God or laws about society, but to experience with men and women before us the way God spoke to them. We hear his message and we hear how the word—the terrifying challenge—came to them and how they obeyed, had to obey, and how the word became an overpowering force in their lives. We do not have to dispute with men about doctrines, and we do not have to argue whether this or that church or this or that religion is right; none of that matters. What matters is that people heard the word and tried to live obedient to the light of truth, hope and love in which the living God showed himself.

I like the song "Lead, kindly light, amid th' encircling gloom, . . ." When I sing it I feel that the man who wrote it stands before the eternal Light and seeks guidance as I seek it. This man was a cardinal of the Roman Catholic Church. He became a Roman Catholic because he could not find peace and rest in his faith without the ancient sacred authority of the church behind it and behind his experience of God and Christ.

Very often people say to me, "How can you dare to stand so entirely alone? We need the authority of the Bible and the authority of the church. Our own unaided experience does not give us the strength to risk our lives going on the hard way." But I had to go my way alone. When I was a young pastor, Christ showed me the spiritual distress and loneliness of the German laboring people, people who could not hear the message of Christ because the church defended the oppression under which they suffered. So I had to stand against the majority of the churches and the church people. When I was in distress and did not see what to do, the living Christ was there, and he showed me the next step, the one step needed.

I had to go through many struggles against church authority, tradition and prejudice. No words of the church, no explanations of theologians made my way clear. He himself spoke to me. Jesus of Nazareth became the message of God for me today. He taught me to accept my cross; he made me certain of his resurrection; he made me strong to stand alone. After a life of hardship, lonely struggling and difficulties, came the real decisive question, whether I could stand when all the foundations of life seemed to break and death was imminent.

Not the church, not the poor pastor who visited me in prison, not anything of authority was my help, but the living Christ. He made me clear that his goal is the truth. He made me certain that for me and my children it was better to take suffering than to deny conscience. He makes me certain again today when, in disappointment, I sometimes ask, "For what did we suffer if the people are again going the wrong way?"

I do not deny that people like Newman, the cardinal, can find the reality of Light where I did not find it. I do not deny fellowship to those who follow Christ in other words and doctrines, and who feel called to other tasks. But I often think that very many do not come to the full reality of God because, before they find it, they rest in authority. In catastrophe everything is changing. For millions of people the traditional words and doctrines and images of God are meaningless. How can we bring them the message if we ourselves are bound up in tradition and cannot show them God's presence, as it came to us, in words that make them understand?

We will never come to a full strength in God if we do not acknowledge the sin of our lives. But, for many good Christians, faith is so bound up with tradition that they never realize the deep sinfulness of custom.

Again and again the churches have been the last to see the injustices of tradition. Capitalist organization and technical development brought growing welfare for millions while at the same time it created slavery for other millions. The churches have been very slow. It is hid from their eyes that tradition is not sufficient to give truth and insight, that once more we must stand before God alone and hear his voice.

There are millions who are full of peace and strength because they have found God in tradition and authority. There are millions whose lives go on without consciousness of new need. But there are also millions who have lost the ability to live in old ways. The ethics of the past have become lies to them, its laws injustice, its faith deception. And there are those who see this fact, this need, and are called to seek a new foundation for man's life and work. They are those people to whom God says today, "Get thee out of thy country, and from thy kindred, and from thy father's house, unto a land that I will show thee."

He leads them through despair and loneliness and doubt and error and even through sin and helplessness and darkness. But he gives them new visions, new thoughts, new outlooks—and perhaps the power by which eternal truth again overwhelms the inward being of the millions. "Not by might, nor by power, but by my Spirit, saith the Lord."

At the end of a talk I gave in a German town, a man of perhaps fifty years came to me saying, "I must speak to you in private." We went aside, and he said to me with tears in his eyes, "For many years I have longed, Sunday by Sunday, to go to church to hear the old hymns and to serve God, but it has become impossible for me. When I come near the church, I see standing in the door the field chaplain who was with us in the war, and I hear again the words he said to us in 1914 when we were young men waiting for our first attack. He said, 'Shoot them, beat them, kill them. Win the attack.' So I cannot go into the church."

When the man had left I asked who he was, and I was told that he was chairman of the Communist Party of that district. Here is a man who cannot go into the church, cannot come to the worship of God because between him and the church is the war cry of a Christian pastor. He is one of millions who cannot hear the message. This man, longing for what is eternal, went to the Communist Party. He longs for a world of justice, of peace. He lives in a world of hatred and privilege and oppression. In the Communist Party he hears a loud voice promising him a world of justice, peace and love in which property and economic antagonism can no longer set men against men. He is aware of the message of Christ that violence and hatred are not the right way. But at the same moment he sees Christians prepare for war to defend their privileges and their domination. And then, sad at heart perhaps, he hears alike from Christian pastors and Communist leaders the same hopeless teaching: man is such a wretched, such a sinful, such a greedy being that his passions will never be overcome. Always he will fight before giving up domination, privilege, nationalist ambition.

From both sides the same gospel of despair: in this world you must fight, fight even for the highest purposes. Christians believe that they have not only the right but also the duty to use things like the atomic bomb to realize ideals. And oppressed men conclude that they have not only the right but the duty to fight in the same way for their ideals. Both are so strongly dominated by unhappy experiences with other men, so involved in distrust, that they cannot see the human being in their opponent—the human being who would have no ideals or longing for love and fellowship was not the image of God in his innermost being. Such men dare not trust in the power of God. They have not the courage to speak to that of God in man, that of God in their antagonists. That is why they are helpless to overcome hatred.

Distrust of man is the essence of the outward history of man. History shows clearly that man defends privilege violently and tries violently to free himself from oppression. But for Christians can that be the reality of man and history? I hear the cry of Jesus out of the mouth of all helpless men and women who see no hope for themselves except in force and fighting. But I see great danger when such helpless, faithless people call themselves Christians. Jesus did not ask his followers to fight for him. He did not ask his heavenly Father to send him twelve legions of angels. He went to the cross and suffered, certain that suffering love would overcome the world. And yet Christianity identifies itself with one opposing power or another, not seeking justice but following tradition.

Let us hear the challenge of Christ. There may be hard disappointment and bitter suffering on the road he points to. He never promised quick or easy victory. Only by our suffering can we overcome prejudices bred in millions of people by the inability of Christians to speak to their times. Mahatma Gandhi led a great nation along his way of truth. When will the Christian conscience be strong enough to unite those who call themselves after Jesus in the building of a world of brotherhood? When will we be ashamed to call Christian those who trust in the sword?

## Is God Real? Are We Real?

There were many good Christians, among them pastors and church leaders, who told me when Hitler came to power, "I cannot lose my position since I must care for my children, and they have to continue their education." Or they said, "My son cannot lose his calling. He must say, 'Heil Hitler.' What will he do if he loses his job?" They all thought that material existence was more important than conscience. What was their God? They had an idea of God, but the reality to which they trusted their lives was money and the getting of money.

I speak of Germany. There are today good Christians, pastors and church leaders, who in sermons, articles and pamphlets excuse themselves and their nation. From all history they search out the evil deeds of others and point to every mistake and injustice of other nations. "Look," they say, "they are no better than we are." When they speak of the terrible guilt which the German nation brought on itself during the last century, they look at others and compare themselves. They do not stand before God, and they do not try to bring their nation to stand before God. It seems to me that one of the decisive tasks of Christians in Germany is to bring people to realize the reality of God. If God is reality, then I know that I will never find a good way in the future, not happiness, not strength, until I find his forgiveness and his spirit to begin anew.

So long as God is an idea in which we believe only with the mind, whilst in real life our chief aim is earning money and winning influence and power, we will never overcome the inward weakness that is servility. We will never overcome that outward weakness, nationalism, so long as it is more important to defend the honor of a nation against accusation than to find the right relation to God in our conscience. And it may be that what is true of Germany is true of all mankind.

When we think of the future of our nations, do we trust in God or do we trust in weapons and armies and all the clever arts which have nothing to do with him? Is he real to us at all if, in important problems of life, we do not trust in him? What does it mean, this trusting in God? I think it means that we are certain that spiritual power is life's precious foundation. It means that we are called as nations and as individuals to take a great task, to lose our lives and to find the life and power which overcomes distrust and hatred and cowardice.

We look back to those whom catastrophe destroyed, those who could not live out their lives, those who gave them because they could not submit to that which was against their consciences. They gave their lives because they had heard Christ's challenge. They had to obey. Something of his eternity lived in them and made them forever his fellow workers, even though we cannot realize it now.

For now, when outward improvement comes, guilt and suffering are zealously forgotten. It seems as if poor and empty people will again win leadership and as if the nations will again run the way of momentary power and success. It is utter darkness if out of the catastrophe not only individuals but whole nations go on as poor and empty of spirit as before.

But the challenge of the living Christ is behind catastrophe; it is in it, beside it, through it. We had to suffer and risk our lives, and we have again to suffer and risk our lives in confronting more catastrophe. But by hearing his voice, hearing it in the midst of ruin, obeying his voice, taking our task in suffering, forgetting ourselves and becoming his instruments—thus we become real. His victory comes into our lives because we try to do his work. Eternity is in our lives overcoming fear and hatred, and giving us this great vision: that we are Christ's fellow workers on earth, united with him in his eternal being.

# 3

# OUR HEARTS ARE RESTLESS

*Seek not humility. . . . Seek not for faith to move moun-*
*tains. . . . Seek not pleasure, neither of body nor of soul. . . .*
*Seek not power, not even power to do great deeds. . . . Seek*
*nothing by itself, for whatever it be will destroy itself. Only*
*one thing is to be sought alone. God alone is an end in*
*Himself.*

GILBERT KILPACK

The work of Gilbert Kilpack has been centered upon a faith
that excites, that involves, that shuns the middle roads of caution
and worldly wisdom, and keeps to that narrow, distant, sharp-
lighted road which the great Christian writers and teachers have
sought to follow. The discovery of this path came to him from his
own experience: student ministry in a logging village in Oregon
and in a small town in Ohio during the course of his under-
graduate and graduate study. He was for a year a student at
Pendle Hill, for five years Executive Secretary of the Stoney Run
Friends Meeting in Baltimore. As extension secretary at Pendle
Hill he speaks to groups throughout the country, and as lecturer
he discusses the religious implications of the world's literary
classics. He is the author of various pamphlets, including the
William Penn lecture, *The City of God and the City of Man. Our
Hearts are Restless* appeared in 1946.

The outcome of all human living and thinking depends
upon what we make of the first three chapters of the book of
Genesis. I say this not to astonish nor for the sake of novelty,
but because to miss the implications of these chapters will,
in the end, make all the difference between the Kingdom of
God and the kind of world we make. These chapters tell a

story, and through that story is revealed the agonizing discovery of our human freedom—our freedom to choose between good and evil, and not only freedom to choose, but the imperative laid upon us to choose the good daily or inevitably fall into evil. The fact of our freedom is none other than the fact of our separation from our Creator. God made us for Himself, that is, He made us as a portion of His own eternal Self, extended into earth and time; but we are separated from Him by our knowledge of good and evil, and thus freedom is at once the source of all our dismal failure and the means of all our brightest visions of growth into goodness. Man is separated from God, but secretly united to God; that is the prime fact of life, and all things in all creation speak of this separation, this incompleteness which has infected all.

Man, as a part of creation, says in all his corruption and in all his nobility nothing so absolutely certain as that he is a half-being. And though ideas such as these may seem unimportant in our bustling world, the testimony of seekers after life in all ages is that nothing is so important as the completion of our half-lives, the God-filling of our void. Human problems seem to be solved without this divine second birth, but actually they are only forced out of sight and eventually they appear again in new guise. Everything waits upon the "oneing" of our lives.

"That of God in every man" is as a finger pointing to that of God which is infinitely more than the good in every man. And the first step in our human reformation may well be a growth in sensitivity to that restless questioning in our hearts, that unfinished something in nature which groans in travail, that endless quest for something greater, which runs through history like a golden cord. We shall learn to see through a window which shows us all people and all things in their unfinished state, drawn, however feeble their response, toward their source: Augustine beginning his *Confessions* with the vision that God has made us for Himself and our hearts are restless till we rest in Him; Rousseau beginning his *Émile* with the pronouncement that man was born free but is everywhere in chains; Jesus teaching his divine kingdom through parables; Plato interpreting ancient myths; Ben Jonson finding the soul's thirst which asks a drink divine; George Herbert likening man to a pulley, ever drawing back to God; the scientist trembling before the awful thing he has let loose upon humanity; the artist weeping that he can never fully express his vision: these, and everything that is, both mean and divine, say that God is our goal and destiny, and that without Him there is no meaning. This incompleteness of all life forms itself into a question, a question burning deep in every human life. It steals into every mind, yet few will confess to having heard it, and still fewer will give it a clear answer. In some centuries this question rages among men like wildfire and in others it drops to a tiny glow, but it never ceases; it is always there, burning away with every breath we take. Yet, feverishly and systematically, we turn ourselves from facing up to it.

The question comes unexpectedly to a man riding the early morning bus as some great view opens suddenly before him, but with the slam of his office door it is shut out. The housewife in the midst of her duties is strangely made quiet, but with amazing deftness she finds some chore that might as well be done this moment. The student among his books falls to pondering as the old question appears between the lines, but his professors insist on the written text. The soldier on his lonely watch meditates on death and through the black night of horror lays his hand upon the greater life of all eternity. The conscientious objector lifting the epileptic idiot from his everlasting cot stands face to face with the ancient question—the same one that primitive man heard in the garden. The preacher in the pulpit who suddenly hears his own words for the first time, the rich man building new barns, the philanthropist busy with his good works, the voluptuary enmeshed in his pleasures, the priest reading his prayer book, the Quaker in his meeting house, all, all are brought low for a moment and made to look into the abyss of eternity, to see themselves in the light of that eternity, to ask themselves the old, old question, *Why am I here on this strange earth—what is the point to my life, to any life, to all human life?*

That is the question which passes from soul to soul and which we turn from and even conspire to avoid as one avoids some insidious disease. And truly, society sometimes appears to be a great conspiracy to aid us in escaping the essential. The endless gag programs on the radio, the movies, the narcotic music of the day, the thousand and one social occasions —all are used as so many *outs,* and each man has his favorite *out,* his blinkers with which he keeps out of sight the eternal issue.

I have tried to make words define this elemental question, but somehow words won't do, for it is more than a question; it is a spirit, an attitude of soul which looks upon the world and all creation with great expectancy. It is the doorstep from which one passes into the house of things divine. It is the everlasting thirst expressed by Thoreau when he said that he went to Walden to drive life into a corner and, if it proved sublime, to know it by experience and not by hearsay; it is the persistent voice of the Eternal, crying in man for satisfaction, which alone gives hope to our poor world. Could we by some strange alchemy completely silence this seeking Voice within us, we should have cut the vital life-nerve of humanity and all would surely be lost.

They are honest people who ask themselves whether life is worth living, whether there is anything to get ready for, whether there is anything worth getting ready for. They are probably not pious folk. Pious folk do not easily give way to questions of this kind. For piety and a questioning mind are a rare combination, one which is costly, and a very great thing. So this question is pondered by the free, the inquiring person. The settled "religious" individual feels certain that all is well with his soul and does not care to be disturbed.

Probably those who are filled with doubt but keep seeking and those who sin but despise their sinning are nearer the Kingdom than "religious" folk who rest content, who have stopped seeking and expecting greater things from God; for our salvation lies in giving way daily to the seekings, promptings, and questionings which assail us from within. Those who give way daily, find themselves in a brotherhood which cuts across church and cultural divisions, for they are led by the God of all, and they feel with George Fox that a new spirit is arising which will make the nations like waters.

But ours is an age neither of deep piety nor of rank scepticism. It will, I believe, increasingly be seen that the average soul of our day is simply a blank check, religiously speaking. He is not devoutly Christian like one set of grandparents, nor a free thinker like the other, nor is he lukewarm like his parents; he simply has no spiritual heritage. The wheel of history has turned its awful revolution and brought up this new nonentity, but if he is human at all, he inwardly, secretly hungers for a life of faith, a faith that will burn like an ever increasing flame revealing the heart of the Eternal Being.

What is the point to my life, and to all life on earth? I cannot answer this question by means of clear, convincing logic. I do not believe that there is what can be called a rational answer. The question itself is an intimation that can be satisfied only by an experimental life of faith and love. It is an intimation that life must hold something great, that ordinary humdrum life should open upon exalted vistas, that life teems with potentialities if only we can get ready to receive it. Such intimations are seeds of divine truth; plant them, nurture them, let them grow, and they will blossom into a life which will more than answer all our incoherent questionings.

A Man went out into the wilderness, not only to face the *essential*, but to wrestle with it; that is, he wrestled with every possible *evasion* of the essential question, and with every false and easy answer to it that we have used in the centuries since. We have no more exceeded his temptations than we have exceeded his goodness. All the confessions ever written by saints and sinners are but commentaries upon his struggle.

The essential, the primal question is simply "that of God in every man" seeking its fulfillment. That there is that of God in every man cannot be affirmed too many times, but it can be affirmed too easily. We should every time we use the expression, be made to stop and think of the strange, terrible, and wonderful implications of such a belief.

We stand as individuals before God who is ever disturbing, prompting, questioning, and laboring with us. Are we ready to give way daily to His unitive healing, both the cauterizing and the anointing?

We stand before our God as an indivisible brotherhood. Are we ready to give up that false freedom and that personal pride which withhold us from the inward unity of mankind? God's gift of free will has made it possible for us to evade this question in comfortable times, but the chaos of our generation has revealed our anarchy in the light of His intention, and now we cannot avoid it. We cannot avoid it for we have a peculiar destiny in the sight of God, a destiny which will not leave us content in such a world. By our spiritual heritage we belong among those people who have left all in search of the Kingdom of Christ, who recognize that this world is not the Kingdom, but who believe that by turning our hearts, minds, and wills to him with heroic persistency we shall begin to live now in the Kingdom. How can the nightmare epoch in which we live fail to arouse us to our condition? How can it fail to make us ask ourselves whether we, as religious groups, are ready to accept our God-intended destiny, and whether as individuals we are ready to be discovered by the love, the truth which has been seeking us everlastingly? Are we ready to accept the awful responsibilities of those who are baptized of the Spirit? Whatever the judgments of men, our hearts tell us we are not ready.

I will tell you plainly why we are not ready to take our part in this drama of the Kingdom, the drama of the Kingdom of God versus the Kingdom of Man, which had its beginnings centuries ago and which in our generation has appeared so terrifying. As individuals we are willing to be ready if only we can be spared the labor of getting ready. We are willing to be reformed if only we can be spared the unsettling disturbance of the process. We want to be spiritually alive, but also to be comfortable; to be prayerful, but not to rise early in the morning to pray; to possess power to lead, but not to undergo the discipline that it takes to control power. We seem to be filled with the desire for contraries and contraries only!

George Meredith has put it facetiously when he says, "In the hundred and fourth chapter of the thirteenth volume of the Book of Egoism, it is written: 'Possession without obligation to the object possessed approaches felicity.'" Do you see? To be counted among the fellowship of those whose destiny is the Kingdom of God, without bearing a cross, is the greatest delight this world offers.

Our common escape from a life of total commitment to

God is to plead the complexity of the modern age. "Life is so complex," we sigh—and proceed on our own sweet complex way. Life has always been complex and always will be complex for those who are divided in heart and will. We may suspect that even St. Anthony alone in the desert lived, when he was divided in his mind, as complex a life as any New Yorker. Ours is a complex age, but to the singlehearted, the complexity of our times is of little consequence. Simplicity is order among diversity. Disorder is confusion over and vacillation between two plain choices. The pure in heart know that when the Kingdom of the Spirit is seen in all its beauty and desired with a single will, then order is brought out of confusion.

What is to be done? The most obvious thing, the hardest thing of all: to begin to live the simple Gospel and to teach the simple Gospel. Religion is on one side complex—richly, divinely complex—as it must be if God is all reality. But within the complex framework of religion *there is a simple Gospel.* The Bible is complicated, but it contains a simple way of life. I say that if we are to be reborn as parts of a religious movement we shall, night and day, have to live, think, pray, and teach the simple gospel of Christianity. We exercise no force in the world because our religion is a muddle in our own minds. Nothing is clear-cut, simple, burning. We are afraid to speak as plainly as the Beatitudes, and also we are unable. Men sold all they possessed and followed Jesus because in a world of complex choices, he stood with a clear and certain voice; there was no doubt where he was going; it was diametrically opposite to the way of the world.

There is a true complexity which comes from an awareness of infinite variety and there is a false complexity which arises out of our squirming and maneuvering to avoid the daily dying-to-the-world element of our faith. We want devotion, but don't want to read *The Bible, The Imitation,* or John Woolman's *Journal* with open minds; we want intelligence but will not fast sufficiently to have a clear mind; we want righteousness but will not arrange our lives for corporate worship more than once every 168 hours; we want truth but will not hunger and thirst for it.

The straight of it is that we are not willing to be ready. We have sought excuses, pleading lack of mental range or native talent. But that will not do, for God asks us to be only what He will make of us. It is plain that the human will is the powerful lever that releases God to work in us. No good pleading: "The spirit is willing but the flesh is weak." Jesus said those words but he did not excuse himself by them. Can we imagine him using them to plead out of his crucifixion? When we will to become a part of a spiritual reformation, God will bring it to pass. When we will it, we shall have life in the Light, not because we have taken thought of it, but because we have prayed that our selfish wills might no longer cover the Light. The Kingdom of God is born on earth *because* we will it, but not by *means* of our will.

Let us see how a fondness for contraries has caused us to set aside ancient testimonies as being too complex for the modern age. We must bear in mind that we are here dealing with symptoms. The primal germ of our failure lies very deep and is inward, but an honest consideration of our outward failure may lead us to the inward source of regeneration.

*We stand for Peace*—but we do not want the things which make for peace. And this is nothing new; Thomas à Kempis said it in a world as war-weary as our own: "All men desire peace but few indeed desire those things which make for peace." We too would like to be counted among those blessed meek—but we also want to possess the earth, we are not content to inherit it. We want peace—but our financial security, our gracious, quiet homes are still dependent upon the industries of war. We know that the roots of war reach into every suburb and every home and that those roots would wither and die if we did not feed them with a publicly accepted everyday brand of human selfishness.

We have been seduced by the vision of a false peace, a very human concoction. I can think of no more awful heresy which has assailed the modern church than the belief that peace can be had on this earth without suffering for it—suffering with the faith that love will surely have the final word, that though we will be crushed to earth, from our final words of forgiveness will arise a new communion of saints who, charged with a yet more glorious celestial contagion, will gather the world into a new brotherhood. *Our heresy is that of having mistaken spiritual lethargy for technical error.* To date we have learned only how to beat our enemy; until we learn how to win him we are doomed to a world of endless wars.

*We stand for Community*—but we do not want the things which make for community, for realization of community means lavishing on others the concern that God has already lavished on us.

Our prophetic historians have long been telling us that cosmopolitanism is a symptom of cultural decay. "Oh," we say, "our cosmopolitanism is marked by greater governmental responsibility than man has ever known before." And here is another heresy, not an abstruse philosophical heresy, but a heresy of life, the belief that large-scale philanthropy and state-directed economic and social responsibility can take the place of the small community unit. Our greatest physical-mental need is not simply to be clothed and fed and to take exercise, but rather to be clothed, fed, and to take exercise in a particular way—as divine-human beings. We must belong to a community which needs us as we need it. In community, true, deep human needs become the business of life, but the world is rapidly moving "out of community"; we are trying to do the job without regard for the person. The rehabilitation of the hackneyed term "brotherhood" is of central importance; the radio church of the air can never take the place of the hard-working fishermen gathered by the fire on the seashore to eat the breakfast prepared for them by loving hands. Somehow it seems that Christ is divisible into millions of small communities if they are truly brotherhoods based on forthright personal relationships, but he is not divisible among even so few as five states where men are only votes, jobs, soldiers, and pensions.

*We stand for Equality*—but we don't want the things that make for equality. Here is a teaching as plain as the nose on your face. "If any man says he loves God and hates his brother he is a liar." "There is that of God in every man." These things we say, and we admire the good old tradition of equality, but a vanishing point is near. Even the memory of that tradition will pass from us if we do not begin to live it boldly. Our failure to live in the spirit of equality is part and parcel with our failure to live in community and at peace. This testimony plagues us constantly today. It is no longer a question of philanthropy, it comes "home to men's business and bosoms" and rankles in us night and day, for our human pride is at stake. Years ago, Olive Schreiner in Africa sensed this strange problem of ours very clearly.

You know up country on the great plains, where the camel thorn trees grow, there are ant heaps as high almost as man.

Millions of ants have worked at them for years, and slowly and slowly they have grown a little and a little higher. Sometimes I have fancied if a little ant should come on the top of one of these heaps, and should rear himself on his hind legs and wave his little antennae in the air, and should look around and say, "My ant heap, that I have made! My ant heap, from which I see so far!—My plains—my sky—my thorn trees—my earth!" and should wave his little antennae and cry, "I am at the beginning of all!" —and then suddenly a gust of wind should come. The ant heap would still be there, the ant heap on the top of which he chanced to be born; there would still be the trees and the plain and the sky; but he would be gone forever.[1]

We stand on the top of our little ant heap of a world, proudly boasting of our culture, waving our little racial flag, and taking for our own all the advantages that the centuries before have given us, forgetting that once another people of another color and another continent stood where we now stand, that they laid the foundation, and will perchance stand on the top again.

*We stand for Simplicity*—but we don't want the things which make for simplicity: frugality, austerity, the giving up of many possessions, plain honest thinking, and above all joy in religion. There is no freedom without simplicity and without freedom there is no joy. To attain to simplicity is first of all to have a single sublime purpose in life, and second it is to order all one's time, thought, and possessions so that they may contribute to, rather than hinder, our progress toward that sublime goal. There is not, of course, much use telling people to be simple; when we pause in our flight from God, He will overcome us and we shall then prize a life of simplicity above all else; we shall wonder then that we ever had time for a life of endless commonplaces.

As it is, Jesus could hardly look upon Christians today and say, "Blessed are ye poor." The loss is ours and the world's, for we can no more possess our souls without simplicity than the world can move forward without a society of the blessed poor. Man was given two hands—one to hold to God and the other to hold to the joys and sorrows of humanity, and if

[1] *From Man to Man*, by Olive Schreiner (New York: Harper & Brothers, 1927), p. 12.

man's hands are loaded with possessions and he is anxious about many things he will serve neither God nor humanity. We say, "Simplicity has become, in this complex world, a relative matter," and so we go on eating our big meals and reading our wordy books. Simplicity is relative? Yes, relative to the needs of the Kingdom. There is a simplicity which is laxity, but those who would live now in the Kingdom need a simplicity which cleaves the good from the evil like a sharp knife. We favor complexity today because it provides such a wide stretch of gray between the white of good and the black of evil. See how we are all content with the gray.

In the back yard of my boyhood home we had a stone bird bath which the birds used regularly and so energetically that the bath often had to be filled twice a day. One morning we looked out of the window and saw a robin fly down to the bath which was at the moment bone dry. The bird perched solemnly on the edge for a moment and then proceeded boldly into the center of the bath where it fluttered vigorously, splashing great imaginary drops of water high into the air. It then proceeded to sit on the edge of the bath and preen itself, and eventually it flew off, no doubt greatly satisfied. Too often our flutterings of activity have no more reality than bathing in an empty bird bath. I do not care whether we are found out, nor do I care whether at any time we seem a failure in the eyes of the world. I dread the truth of the accusation that we have come to our faith easily and without much seeking, that we have, as Charles Péguy would say, pulled our religion out of our overcoat pocket. Each generation must seek out its own salvation in fear and trembling. I have no doubt that if we seek, fearless of consequences, new paths of holy experiment will open before us and we shall again become a movement with the power of sharing the love of God with all men.

There is an inward light and an inward darkness. How

does the light grow in ascendancy over the dark? How do we become children of the light? We are convinced, but how do we become converted? We look at the child in the stable and then turn and look at the figure on the cross of Golgotha and may well ask: "How does one come out of the other?" As a matter of fact we seldom ask this question, for we more often than not take it for granted that great men always have been great, and that saints always have been saints. It is the *becoming* that marks the greatness of the saint and not the achievement or the approbation of the world. Could I say to myself and be convinced of its truth: "Where I stand now in life, St. Francis or John Woolman once stood also," it would be a good thing, but it would be a greater thing if I could realize that where I stand now, St. Francis and John Woolman knelt. They did not kneel in order to become great or blessed, they knelt because they greatly desired the good and gave way to it. They were not good; no man is good in himself; the highest thing that can be said about any human life is that in so far as it is thoughtful of and absorbed with the divine, it takes on the likeness of the divine light which shines through it. Jesus was not exaggerating when he said, "Call no man good," for goodness is of God and if any man seems good it is simply because he greatly desires God's goodness.

The seeds of good and evil are in us all. How does "the secret shining of the seed of God" become a living flame, that we may be filled with light? No one can answer this in full, for each of us must come to God in a private, individual way. Each must seek out his own salvation.

Still, there are certain ancient practices and holy beliefs and experiences which are common to all who come into the life of the Kingdom of God on earth, and therefore we can say without hesitation that to become children of the light we must first of all learn to pray, for as Pascal says: "All the miseries of men arise from not knowing how to be at ease in their closets." I do not care how broad a definition one gives to prayer so long as one does not impose a humanly fabricated limitation upon the possibilities of prayer. I cannot do without the faith that prayer is an openness, an attentiveness to God which lifts one to an ever enlarging horizon revealing His goodness and truth.

As we look at the great heritage of mystical literature we see that it is little more than the art of learning to pray. There are those who say, "I am not a mystic," in the same way they would say, "I do not have rosy cheeks," or "I don't care for boiled onions," or "the music of Stravinsky doesn't appeal to me." We are all born with differing spiritual traits, differing talents, and differing capacities, physical and mental. Yet I firmly believe that we are all of us born with some capacity for prayer, and that with all of us the capacity is greater than we think. How do we come by the notion that we can prejudge our capacity for God? Prayer is essentially *not* prejudging what He can do with us and through us.

The mystic is not one who possesses a special power to invade the Divine; rather he is any ordinary person who persistently puts down his human pride so that the Divine may invade him. The worldly man is the one who has learned to sidestep the everlasting seekings of God's truth; the mystic is the one who has learned *not* to sidestep. Anyone can become a worldly soul and anyone can become a Godlike soul. I never know whether or not I am a mystic until I bend my knees, which are not so much stiff as stubborn, until I bow my head, which is not so much filled with lofty reasoning as with lofty pride, until I calmly fold my hands, which are more restless from anxiety than from a desire to serve.

I say a bold thing. There are but two kinds of people in this world: those who pray and those who do not pray. This

classification cuts deep. And note—this is terribly important
—I do not say that those who pray are good, that those who
do not pray are bad, for such a distinction is foreign to the
primitive Christian teaching. Charles Péguy has reminded us
prophetically, "A Christian is not defined by a low water
mark, but by communion. One is not a Christian because of
standing at a certain moral, intellectual, even spiritual level."
He continues, "One is a Christian because of belonging to a
certain ascending race, a certain mystic race, temporal and
eternal, belonging to a certain kindred. This cardinal classification cannot be made horizontally, but vertically." Thus
it is that Augustine could say that "the Apostles were de-
feated by the robber who then believed when they failed."
The Apostles were "good" persons turned in the wrong direction through their failure to persist in prayer; the thief
was a "bad" person who lifted his head toward God, who in
his agony turned his will toward God and who thus moved
into God's universal stream of truth. The church of today is
largely made up of good people who are turned in the wrong
direction; they have retained a formal goodness, but through
their failure to persist in an inward attentiveness to God
they have removed themselves from His Presence and are
blind to His ongoing truth. And so we can make the cardinal
distinction between those who pray and those who do not,
and it is a distinction that goes to the source of all human
failure.

In speaking of the life of prayer I do not hold up for your
example those persons who seem to have a special gift for
seeing beyond, nor those who are always receiving visions. I
rather hold up the Christ who sweats drops of blood to bring
his will under the will of the Eternal Father. He did not in
his awful hour pray for special graces, miraculous powers, or
sight into the future; he sought only to make God's will his,
and we can pray no better.

There are many modern devotees who look upon prayer mainly as a means of integrating the human personality, a sort of inward "knowing of thyself." But to start with man is to start at the wrong end and will not bring us to true prayer. Pascal says: "Amongst other astonishing facts of the Christian religion, this is one, that it reconciles man to himself in reconciling him to God." Now it is precisely the reverse of this that many hold to be prayer. Too often we try to know God through the reconciliation of self with self. This will not do, for it is the fact, the experience of God that counts; the God who shines within us is also the great outflowing source of all light. We cannot do without an object of worship, and nothing separates us from the awareness of this source of all light but our own self-sufficiency. There is no good in claiming constitutional difference; it is not a matter of intellect, but of will. Nor is it a matter of *feeling* prayerful, for the test of prayer is not the pleasure or feeling we have of God, but rather the agility with which we will His will, and the confidence we place in Him.

The Christian life [says Fénelon] is a long and continual tendency of our hearts towards that eternal goodness which we desire on earth. All our happiness consists in thirsting for it. Now this thirst is prayer. Ever desire to approach your Creator, and you will never cease to pray. . . . Do not think that it is necessary to pronounce many words. To pray is to say, Let Thy will be done; it is to form a good purpose; it is to raise your heart to God; it is to lament your weakness, it is to sigh at the recollection of your frequent disobedience. This prayer demands neither method, nor science, nor reasoning; it is not necessary to quit one's employment; it is a simple movement of the heart toward its Creator, and a desire, that whatever you are doing, you may do it to His glory. The best of all prayers is to act with a pure intention and with a continual reference to the will of God.

This, I believe, is the best kind of prayer; it sounds so simple, so desirable and yet it has proved to be the most difficult and the least often attained. This type of prayer is a goal, and techniques and methods of devotion are not to be shunned in attaining to it, though all particular forms of devotional exercise must be kept flexible. If you ask, "Is it not enough simply to love God?" I can answer yes, it is enough, but love includes and embraces all systems of religious exercise in itself. I quite agree with Frederick Faber at this point. He says,

There is something intensely sickly about the spiritual life. It is nothing but unbandaging, examining sores, bandaging them up again, smelling salts, rooms with blinds down, and I know not what dishonourable invalidisms and tottering convalescences. It seems to me no slight temptation to love God with a headlong love, in order that one's soul may not be sickened with these degrading symptoms or valetudinarian sensations of the spiritual life, but live a robust, out-of-doors kind of religious existence.

There is no substitute for a "headlong love," but for most of us, love—even a grand, overpowering love—without regular devotional customs, makes for a somewhat spasmodic religious life. One cannot think of many saints who attained to a high degree of attentiveness, that is, a sustained love of God, without devising some method of recalling themselves to the presence of God in those moments and days of interior torpor which hit all of us. Forgetfulness seems a small enough human defection, and yet without regular devotional practices, what a great obstacle forgetfulness becomes in our life of prayer. How quickly we forget the good words of a friend, spoken only yesterday; the words from the Bible read but last night, and even the pure visitations of the Spirit of this morning fade without constant recollection. We are the inheritors of a Kingdom, but we receive our inheritance only as we have the will to practice receiving it daily.

Preparation for prayer is then first of all the art of recollection, a calling to mind those experiences and facts of God which are most apt to lead us into His presence, and it is this act which gives meaning to all of life. The degraded person is one in whom the powers of recollection are so lost that he no longer *sees* a sunset, and still less does he remember that only yesterday he was born into this world out of a shadowy nothingness and that tomorrow he must depart into the unknown. But with those who practice the art of recollection a breath of fresh air is more wonderful than all the inventions of man, for the breath of fresh air, or the meanest flower that blows is referred to the Source of all, and life is then seen in its true proportions. It was the discovery of this practice which saved Tolstoy from possible suicide. Walking despondent in the forest he suddenly became aware that as often as there came to mind the very word *God,* a sense of hope, a feeling of life surged through him. And he said to himself, "Why do I look farther? He is there: He, *without whom one cannot live.* To acknowledge God and to live are one and the same thing. God is what life is. Well, then! Live, seek God, and there will be no life without him." In *Anna Karenina,* Levine labors all day in the fields cutting grain with peasants and at night he sleeps in the open country under the star-lit heavens, where he receives a great mystical experience of the overflowing goodness of life. But he has enough wisdom to recognize that this feeling will not last for long, that he will soon, as of old, give way to impatience and irritability. This is one of the hardest lessons we learn, that the true spiritual life is not made up of continuous pleasurable feelings. He who would turn to God only when he *feels* God's presence is, as Fenelon says, like one who would live on a diet of milk. Many times we must chew the dry crust. Inward growth comes through two processes which are complementary and indispensable. They might be called the *deflation* and the *inflation* of our human spirits. We are inflated when the infinite source of all goodness bends down and touches our poor lives, giving all the world a new light and a new smell. But this cannot last for long, not yet, for we are not able to bear His love for long; we must be deflated, brought low and made to look into the abyss of human aloneness and human weakness, before we can rise again to bear His love a little longer. And let no one think that the times of deflation when we must practice patience and recollection in the dark, are in any way times less profitable or inferior to the times of great certainty.

This is the way of growth and the only certain thing about it is that it is slow. Faber says well that "Speed, in spiritual matters, is always followed by darkness." And how can it be other than slow, considering that we are seeking so great a thing as the divinization of our whole creaturely beings? I read many years ago a strange passage in Swedenborg, in which the angels in heaven are represented as inspecting a human body from which the spirit has departed. To *their* eyes, every muscle, every nerve, every drop of blood in that body speaks of the selfishness and pride, the love and humility which were the life that once inhabited the body. I think that I see now great truth in that strange passage. Just as a woolen coat in time takes on the shape of the body which wears it, so the body takes on the shape of the soul within it. But only "angel eyes" can see the true correspondence between body and soul. Those who looked upon Father Damien with the eyes of the world saw only a loathesome person of decaying flesh, but with those who felt his inward spirit, even his miserable body revealed the glory of God. Thus our bodies may be broken and scarred, but our souls clean and erect. Here then is what is going on when we pray. The love of God is being poured into every drop of blood in our veins; self-will is being driven out of every nerve; every muscle is learning to respond to His truth and every tissue is being disciplined to proclaim His glory. It is no wonder that prayer is an agonizing thing and that it releases us at one level and leaves us exhausted at another. The battle to make our will the will of God must take its toll. And so Jesus leaves the Garden of Gethsemane completely at one with the way of his Father—but with drops of blood on his brow.

Thus the person steeped in prayer cannot be taken by surprise, or found off guard, for he is conditioned through and through. "It's not a matter of intellect or logic," says Dostoievsky, "It's loving with one's inside, with one's stomach." To love with one's surface mind is something, but only a start; to love with one's involuntary reflexes is a very great thing and not to be accomplished without much travail. St. Catherine of Genoa, who lived at once a life of perpetual inward prayer and great outward activity, could say that the soul "is so full of peace that though she press her flesh, her nerves, her bones, no other thing comes forth from them but peace." The peace she here speaks of is not the peace of a life removed from outward disturbance. It is the peace of a life so conditioned by God that the inevitable disturbances of a life no longer come as a disruptive force. A peace won without much patience and inward suffering is not worth the asking. To resign one's self to the fact that one must travel much in the dark, and be greatly sifted and tossed about is an inevitable step in the way of spiritual growth. To be impatient with one's slow improvement, to whine for more light, to blame one's circumstances, to hope to get beyond travail—all are signs of pride, and indicate a failure to recognize that the moment one consciously turns to the goal of light, one is confronted with a whole new set of temptations. Seek God we must, with a headlong love, with enthusiasm and romantic ardor, but *also* with lowliness and patience, and that is a hard combination.

There is an old story which claims to explain the difference between the Roman and the Celtic tonsure. The Roman monks, so the legend goes, shaved their heads around the sides, so that when the monks knelt in prayer the light streaming through the chapel windows would make a halo effect about their heads. The Celtic monks shaved their heads on top, so that when they knelt in prayer God could look straight down into their souls. We, like the Roman monks, often forget that the object of worship is the loss of self will in the glorification of God, and not the reverse. How tempting it is to use God as a miserable little secret halo for self-will. If we fail to recognize this pitfall we shall make out poorly in the way of prayer.

I have said that one of the first steps in preparation for prayer is the storing up of our lives with the rich experiences of the devout persons of all ages, so that when we practice recollection, there will be a wealth of malleable material to draw upon; the Spirit does not work in a void. Yet in preparation for prayer there is something more decisive than recollection; the whole temper of our ordinary routine life prior to the time of prayer is of first importance. That is why Jesus said, in effect, if you are on your way to the place of worship for a nice hour of peaceful contemplation and you suddenly remember that you carried scandal last week to your neighbor, go and make it right, if it is possible, and then return and your meditation will be good. But if you do not, you may be guilty of the double sin of making prayer an escape from the consequences of evil. True prayer lifts us above our problems, but it does not cover over our sins. In Crevecoeur there is a description of the way the bee stings to death any foreign creature which gets into the hive. If the foreign object is too large to be carried out, such as a snake, then the bees make an airtight, beeswax covering over the object so that its putrefaction will not spoil the honey. We

have no such airtight system for covering up "foreign creatures" in our lives. We may succeed in pushing evil out of
sight and even forgetting it, but it is bound to "smell up"
our prayer lives.

Prayer is of one piece with all life. And the only point in
particular systems of prayer and special times of meditation
is to lead us to that prayer which is continuous, that prayer
which is an everlasting spontaneous inward confidence in
God. We are called to become an inward people who have
passed from endless talk about prayer to the life of prayer.
There are arguments for prayer, but they do not matter
much; what does matter is the life in which prayer has become as central as the marrow in our bones; such a life is the
hand of God in the world. As Meister Eckhart could say that
"not all the saints in heaven nor all the preaching friars and
barefoot monks on earth can stand against one man moved
by the truth," so we dare say that not all the kingdoms of
our world can stand against us if we be grounded in the confidence, the wisdom and the love of prayer—and this is no
small thing.

We shall not be prepared to travel with certainty into the
dark years which are rolling down upon us unless we travel
with the principle of the cross. It is not a dogmatic formula,
not a success recipe; it is an act of faith and love, a belief that
Jesus overcame evil with good and that there is no other
way for us. The principle of the cross is not a system for getting this reform or that; it offers success only in the light of
eternity—and what other light is there? It offers the faith
that evil forces in ourselves and in others can be met with
love, patience, and humility, in spite of contrary instincts, in
spite of social customs and governmental orders. Worldly
persons judge nations and persons by outward forms; God
judges by the inward intent. To the lover of the cross it is

as nothing that the outward form is destroyed so long as the intention of the heart remains pure. God can raise up new bodies, new cathedrals, new cities if our will is in His possession, but what can He do with strong bodies, proud churches, and great cities from which the heart of love has departed?

Of all the miseries incident to man, I can think of no object more deplorable, or more pitiable than that of professed Christians on whom the cross is laid, but who are ignorant of its value; persons who smart under its rigour, who sink beneath its weight but will not be freed from the entanglements of self by means of it. "Recollect," says St. Marthe of Port Royal, "it is the sickness of the soul, not the heaviness of the cross, which makes it hard to bear." And the Mère Angelique of the same religious community has said,

How lamentable it is, that there are so many persons who would rather expose themselves to sin than to inconvenience! They fear to live without health, and they do not fear to live without grace. Souls which seem to belong to God, have almost all a back door, through which to escape when trials press on them.

If you tell me that history and technology have outmoded suffering, I can only reply that narcotics may ease us into this world and ease us out of it, but there can be no easing into the Kingdom of Christ. He suffered supremely to become what he was, and to be his followers we can in no wise escape his suffering of the Garden where human will was beaten down with drops of blood and divine will made to reign over all. The principle of the Cross is no artificial penance, no self-laceration; it is the natural medicine of God for the wounds of life. It is not a dramatic stand, but the secret, daily dying to self; for, as Charles de Foucauld says, "far from us, above all, be those little sorrows, less easy to endure than the great ones, those wounds so paltry, so peevish, so

venomous, wrought by the passions, and by self-love! It is
the shame of mankind to suffer so much for so little."

Elias Hicks said in his *Journal*:

> True Christianity is nothing else than a real and complete
> mortification of our own wills, and a full and final annihilation
> of all self-exaltation. . . . Therefore none are any further Chris-
> tians than as they experience the self-denial, meekness, humility,
> and gentleness of Christ, ruling and reigning in them, so as to
> become their real life.

The principle of the cross is then first of all a daily practice.
It is the ascetic element in our religion without which mystic
faith becomes like weak gruel.

The cross stands squarely in the midst of each day's activities and we make no progress in ourselves or in the world
except through that cross, whose lovers see it implanted in
all things—in the wisp of smoke, in the branches of a tree,
and in the body of man himself. Fritz Eichenberg has done
a powerful wood engraving of Abraham Lincoln. He has
portrayed the holy gleam of compassion through suffering
in that great man's eyes by means of a cross. And this cross
which seems the sorrow of mankind is really its joy, for joy is
not concerned with pain or pleasure; it is blessedness. And
blessedness is God's gift to those who take up the cross of
daily dying to self-will. We have all become solemnly conscious of the world's burden, but let us not suppose we can
avoid our own cross by taking up the world's. Strangely,
God's will for the world is advanced only as we bear our own
cross first.

Suffering is at the heart of Christianity precisely because
Christianity is an incarnational faith. If our goal were to
escape the world of flesh and time, then the cross would be
useless. But the glory of Christianity is the glory of the Spirit
become flesh. The Spirit battles with the flesh not in order to
conquer and kill, but to conquer and bless. We live in a
world of books and buildings, children and cities—these

things are not eternal, they will certainly perish, and yet our eternalness depends upon them. For the benediction of God is upon us as we let Him into books and buildings, children and cities. It is all very well for Whittier to say that "Art builds on sand," but it is only a half-truth. The outward forms of art do perish; books are burned and cathedrals bombed, but men of all ages have borne the cross of self-denial in their hearts to bring this art into being; in anguish they have forged out their eternality *through* the stuff of this world. In this mysterious time of probation, when we carry bodies about with our spirits, that is our lot, our sorrow, and our joy. Through the human suffering of Christ we are brought to eternality. The grain of wheat falls into the earth and perishes, not that it may escape being a grain of wheat, but that the glory of God may be revealed in the next summer's field of waving grain.

As Christians we will have to die to our pride of lineage, forfeit our respectability, embrace the shame of the cross if we would play our part in the drama of the incarnation. The eleventh chapter of the second book of *Imitation* must be turned into a prayer and become our confession: Forgive us, oh God, that we are lovers of Thy heaven but not bearers of Thy Son's cross; that we willingly share his comforts but not his distress; that we are companions of his table but forget his hours of abstinence; that we rejoice with him but will not sorrow with him; that we follow him to the breaking of bread but not to the drinking of his bitter cup; that we seem to be his disciples while we are free from adversity but slacken in devotion and confidence when tribulation comes, sinking into murmuring or despair. For all this forgive us, and teach us to bear our cross through Thy power. Amen.

The *Imitation* says, "They who love Jesus for Himself, and not for their own comfort, will bless Him in the depths of distress." And this leads us to another great Christian teaching without which we can expect no great spiritual awakening. It is simply *that God is to be sought and loved for Himself*. There can be no ulterior motive in our devotion to Him. This sounds like a most elementary admonition, yet it stands at the pinnacle of all the contemplations of the saints. It sounds far removed from the active side of religion, but it is the great fact of religion without which the best laid schemes of reform turn into arrogant delusions. God is not to be called in as the patron of our social, political, economic plans. He is not above these, nothing is too lowly for Him, not even politics, but we shall never find His will in these matters until we come to Him for no reason but Himself.

The end of all life is everlasting growth into God. This is a fact which embarrasses the modern mind, for we find it much more to the point—and, incidentally, much easier— to demonstrate our religion by building more churches, sponsoring bigger campaigns, financing larger charities, and preaching more eloquent sermons than we do by putting ourselves without reserve into the hands of the living God. I do not say that God utterly spurns our strange, mixed motives of worship; I only say that our human restlessness can never be assuaged until we begin to seek Him for Himself. All other goals, no matter how idealistic, are half-way goals and can never fulfill our divine-human destiny.

Seek nothing uppermost in your heart but God only.

Seek not humility. Seek God. Through God you will find humility. Sought as an end, humility will run in a circle and bring you directly back to pride.

Seek not for faith to move mountains. Seek God first. Perhaps the mountains do not need moving; perhaps He will lift you up above mountains, which may be better than moving them.

Seek not pleasure, neither of body nor of soul. This too is

a gift, eluding those who seek it. Seek God, for He alone is able to give joy, which is infinitely finer than pleasure.

Seek not power, not even power to do great deeds. Seek God and Him alone, and power will flow from you in ways and times which are hidden from you.

Seek not any one thing alone; seek not justice alone, for lacking mercy justice will fall by the way; seek not pity alone, for lacking wisdom pity will turn soft; seek not to become harmless as a dove without becoming wise as a serpent, nor wise as a serpent without becoming harmless as a dove. Seek nothing by itself, for whatever it be it will destroy itself.

Only one thing is to be sought alone. God alone is an end in Himself. He holds all means and all ends within Himself. One can seek Him alone and not be afraid. Seek Him alone and all else shall be added; He has promised, and it shall be so.

The most awful calamity which can befall our churches is not a split in the unity of organization, not a loss of social prestige, not persecution by civil authorities, not loss of all our wealth. It is rather the subtle, unseen, slow, everyday weakening of our practice of absolute devotion. The conclusion and summit of the Sermon on the Mount is the admonition to be perfect as our Father in Heaven is perfect. It can hardly be supposed that Jesus was thinking of a perfection of endless minutiae of outward conduct; it was against such that he revolted; such perfection shall be exceeded by striving for an inward perfection of the will. He came not to remove the rigours of religion but to teach a more rigorous way, starting from within, and thus he saved his followers forever from the pride of achievement. Absolute, perfect devotion is a goal, the goal of all life, to grow into God and be as He is, yet a goal to be striven for each hour as though obtainable within the day. Perfection is that Kingdom of

God which never *is* in its fullness on earth, yet is always becoming.

Christian civilization cannot long continue without there dwelling at its heart communities of inward people who persist in making God the measure of all things. Everywhere people cry out for such a brotherhood, even though they will not join with it. That "new and living way that makes the nations like waters" and which enables us to stand fast, the waves breaking over our heads, is not a faint hope or a grand surmise; it is the Divine Imperative. We may fail it, but it cannot perish, for somewhere the absolute voice of God will be heard and our everlasting spiritual lineage will be reborn. This way is hard. Yet God never expects of us more than He is able to do through us. Our cure is hard because our need is desperate. And why He must, to make progress in this world, wring both joy and sorrow from our hearts is one of the great mysteries of faith.

# 4

# THE QUAKER DOCTRINE OF
# INWARD PEACE

*It is not through a struggle to possess the Light, but rather
by permitting the Light to possess us that inner darkness is
overcome.*

## HOWARD H. BRINTON

Howard H. Brinton, one of today's outstanding Quaker
thinkers, is a physicist who became a philosopher and a mathema-
tician who became a mystic. While carrying on child feeding
programs in Germany for the American Friends Service Committee after the first World War, he was struck by the writing of
the seventeenth-century mystic, Jacob Boehme. His thought and
his work began to gravitate toward the inward content of religion. In 1928 he became Professor of Religion at Mills College
and two years later published his study of Boehme, *The Mystic
Will.* Since 1936 Howard Brinton has been Director of Pendle
Hill. His most important written contributions have been *Creative Worship,* a study of the most fruitful occasions for an interplay between the human and the divine, *Divine-Human Society,*
a discussion of the bases of community, and *Quaker Education.*
*The Quaker Doctrine of Inward Peace* appeared in 1948.

We are all suffering from a sense of pressure. Feeling that
our ancestors had ways of meeting the pressures of their day,
we sometimes imagine that we might imitate their ways with
profit. But it may be that their situation was so different
from ours that we cannot imitate them. It is probable that
we are living in an environment which exerts more pressure
on us than was exerted by their environment upon them.

95

The difference between four miles an hour in a buggy and forty miles an hour in an automobile measures in some degree the difference between the speed of living a century or more ago and the present speed. It is an astonishing fact that most of our labor saving devices have not saved us any labor. They have merely increased the number of things which we do. Because our friends can reach us easily on the telephone we are the helpless, obedient slaves of the telephone bell whose demands can no more be disobeyed than can the edict of a dictator. Because we can go anywhere easily and quickly, we go, believing that, as long as we are in motion, something is being accomplished.

But we cannot blame our increased restlessness entirely on the new tools which the restlessness uses to express itself. Some other force is obviously at work. We are busier than we used to be even when we use ancient tools and methods. We are busier because we want to be busier. Why is this? Our gadgets could save us work if we wanted them to do so. Think how much backbreaking labor on the farm would have been saved by our ancestors if they had had our tools without our restlessness.

We sometimes hear a psychological explanation which undoubtedly contains some truth. Busyness, restlessness, the desire for activity is a form of escapism; we are trying to escape from ourselves. Not being able to face our own inner lives with all their stresses and strains, their disorder and chaos, we occupy ourselves as much as possible with what is outward. We do not like our own company so we feverishly seek the company of others. We compensate for inner weakness by seeking outward sources of strength. We are continuously in motion because we do not know what to do when we are still.

But this type of explanation, however true and useful, does not take us very far. In the first place the activist can and usually does reverse it, declaring that all attempts at inward development are forms of escapism. Why should anyone stand still and retreat into himself when there is so much to be done, unless he is afraid of facing the world, unless its problems are too difficult for him to solve? And in the second place this psychological explanation leaves unanswered the question as to why our inner life is so weak or disordered that we fear to face it and so seek relief in outward activity.

There is a partial explanation of our inner disorder which is based on the fact that our interests are spread out over a number of fields in which the standards of behavior are not consistent with one another. Our home creates one set of requirements, our social club another, our meeting for worship another, our business or the business on which we are dependent another. In each case we attempt to fit ourselves into the code of behavior of a certain group of persons and this code may be and often is different from the code of other groups. The standard of behavior in our religious group for instance may be quite different from the standard in our business group. The result is an inner strain. While present in a given group we suppress the standards of the other groups, but we do not eliminate them entirely from our minds. A sense of pressure and tension results. Our ancestors were better integrated within themselves because their lives were better integrated without; they belonged to fewer different kinds of groups. In early Pennsylvania, for example, everything, whether spiritual, intellectual or economic, centered in the Quaker meeting, a condition which made possible an inner life in which there were few conflicting interests.

The activist who seeks explanations based on outer facts declares that our restlessness is due to the terrible state of the world at present. If we could just get the outer world in order we could then feel inward peace. But perhaps he has not the whole truth, perhaps the more fundamental difficulty is with our inward world. As long as there is inward chaos, all outward actions will be contaminated by this chaos. In such a case all that we do will promote rather than allay confusion. We seek to bring peace in the world when there is no peace in our hearts and as a result we infect the outer world with our inner conflict. As an old Chinese saying has it, "The right action performed by the wrong man is the wrong action."

Such inward references are typical of the teachings of Jesus. He had little to say regarding better laws, better governments, better agreements between nations to keep the peace, better organized relief work. "First be reconciled to thy brother and then come and offer thy gift." "Ye have heard that it was said by them of old time—Thou shalt not kill—but I say unto you that whosoever is angry with his brother . . ." and so on through the whole gospel. Such an inward emphasis is also the principal characteristic of Quakerism. For the Quaker, outward and inward combine in an intimate organic relation, but the inward is primary. Accordingly, when we speak of the Quaker way of meeting pressures we must expect that the answer will mainly concern our inward life and only secondarily the changes which we can produce in the outer world. If a tire is too soft we say that the outer pressure is greater than the inner pressure and we remedy the difficulty by increasing the inner pressure. It would be possible to inflate the tire by lessening the outer pressure, but this could be done only under highly specialized conditions. Nor do we meet this problem of the soft tire by going ahead of the car with tools to make the road smoother. Rather we increase the inner pressure so that all jars, bumps, sudden stops or starts can be bearably dealt with.

In similar fashion a person in danger of being overwhelmed

by outside pressures can meet them best by increasing his inner dimensions. He can of course try the other plan: creating changes in his environment in order to reduce the pressures. In the course of such efforts men have contrived a vast array of tools and scientific instruments with which great changes have been brought about in the outer world. We are able to control almost everything except the weather and we seem to be on the verge of controlling that. But one very important element has been left out: we have not succeeded in controlling ourselves. We are still ill at ease, restless, unsatisfied, driven to increasing activity by every new invention. We overlook the all-important alternative to outer change, the increase of our inner resources, our inner strength and stability. Only so can we balance the outer forces and meet every jar and bump on the road with a power which holds its own, which may give way a little only to assert itself the more.

This then is the first answer which we propose to the problem: so to order the inner life that outer pressures can be adequately met and dealt with. This is not the method of the ascetic who conquers his sensual desires by violence toward himself, nor of the hermit who avoids his fellow men, nor of the stoic who makes himself independent and indifferent to the world around him. It is rather an ordering of the inner life, so that there will be a proper balance of inner and outer, the inner holding first place. In one sense we become independent of outer tumults and conflicts, but in another sense we are not independent because we must seek to reproduce in the world around us the inner peace created within ourselves. If we do not seek to reproduce our inner peace it will become lifeless and static.

## The Attainability of Inner Peace

But is inner peace, free from all sense of pressure, attainable? Many would say no. We have a physical body whose demands are insatiable and frequently quite at variance with the standards of the society in which we move. Also we are bound by many ties to a world around us which is in a state of conflict. We should not, even if we could, sever our ties with it. We cannot turn a deaf ear to the cries of suffering around us which disturb our peace.

This question as to the attainability of inner peace is closely related to one of the many issues in the seventeenth century between the early Friends and the Puritans. The Quakers maintained that perfection and freedom from a sense of guilt resulting in complete peace within could be attained. The Puritans held that perfection and its consequent inner peace and freedom were not attainable. To support their view the Quakers quoted such scripture as this: "Mark the perfect man, his end is peace," "Be perfect . . . be of one mind, live in peace," "Now the God of peace . . . make you perfect," "Until we all come . . . unto a perfect man, unto the measure of the stature of the fullness of Christ." There can be little doubt that early Christianity accepted the doctrine of the possibility of human perfection here and now, in this present life.

But for the Puritans and for many modern theologians man can never be free from sin and should therefore never be free from a sense of guilt. He is born in sin, they say, and remains in sin just as long as he is a part of a sinful fleshly world. The penalty may be removed by an undeserved miracle of divine grace, but the sin remains. Christ was perfect, but his perfection is wholly beyond our human reach. Though his life is our ideal, it is not an attainable ideal.

It would be interesting to speculate as to how much of our modern restlessness is due to our Puritan inheritance which demands a perpetual tension between the real and the ideal. Though Quakerism was, about the beginning of the eighteenth century, more influential than Puritanism in colonial America, immediately thereafter Puritanism increased while Quakerism decreased. The new oncoming mechanical age with its outward orientation was less congenial to Quakerism with its inwardly directed spirit. As a result of being outwardly directed, the human soul tended to become reduced to the level of outward nature. Humanity united inseparably with the unceasing flux of material nature and sensual desire. Postponing to the next world the goal of peace and freedom from guilt, the human soul was doomed to restlessness, to the hopeless search for the unattainable. The Absolute vanished leaving only the relative. The goal receded into infinite distance leaving only means and tools. Modern man became a worshipper of tools. His philosophy became pragmatism. By removing peace and perfectability from all things this side of the grave, the Puritans doomed themselves to continual dissatisfaction and frustration, their only hope of salvation being a promise set forth for them in a sacred book. Their descendants built a great material structure in which the human soul wanders homeless and without peace.

George Fox had many arguments with the Puritans on the possibility of peace and perfection in this life. To some who "pleaded for sin" as he expressed it, he said, "If your faith be true it will give you victory over sin and the devil and purify your hearts and consciences," and to others who said, "we must always be striving" he replied, "it is a sad and comfortless sort of striving, to strive with a belief we should never overcome."

His assertion of the possibility of perfection and inward peace may seem at first sight to be based on pride and egotism but the opposite is in reality the case. Its basis is the possibility of complete obedience to the will of God in humility and self-surrender. For the Quaker, perfection and its consequent inner peace can be reached when all of God's immediate requirements as understood are faithfully met. These requirements are never so great that the individual cannot meet them. God requires more of a man than of a boy, more of a saint than of a sinner. Robert Barclay, the greatest Quaker theologian, calls this "a perfection proportionable and answerable to man's measure whereby we are kept from transgressing the law of God and enabled to answer what he requires of us, even as he that improved his two talents so as to make of them four perfected his work . . . no less than he that made of his five, ten." As we are faithful to the light that we have, more will be given. Thus a soldier whose conscience tells him to fight must fight or be a coward. But if he is faithful to the very best that is given to him from on High and endeavors through prayer and worship to increase his sensitivity to the will of God, he will eventually learn another and better way. "There is a growing in the life even where the heart is purified from sin, even as Christ did grow and wax strong in spirit, for a state of perfection doth not exclude degrees."

Inner peace comes through obedience to the Divine Voice not, as Jesus pointed out, blindly as a slave obeys a master, but as a friend complies with the wishes of his friend because the two are one in spirit. "Henceforth I call you not servants but friends for the servant knoweth not what his master doeth."

*Perfection and Pacifism*

An important element in this doctrine of inward peace and its relation to what is somewhat misleadingly called "perfectionism" is indicated in the setting of Jesus' saying "Be ye perfect even as your Father which is in heaven is perfect." Jesus begins by saying, "Love your enemies" and ends by saying that this kind of perfection which is characteristic of God, who makes "his sun to rise both on the evil and on the good," is possible for men also. To be "perfect" is to love your enemies for only by loving your enemies can you remove an inner source of conflict which prevents inner peace. He alone can secure inner peace who is at peace with the world around him even though the world around him may not be at peace with him. Hatred, persecution, cursing (I quote Jesus' list) are expressions of inner disorder. Remove them and peace results; with it will come a sense of achieving that perfection which is characteristic of God who is kind to the evil. No man hates others without a sense of guilt, for in hating others he projects on them a secret, unknown hatred for himself. Love removes this inner conflict which seeks satisfaction in outer conflict. The pacifist is sometimes called a perfectionist. This is true only in the limited sense that he possesses a means of removing that feeling of guilt in himself which generates conflict and hatred and is generated by them. Only when the pacifist attains inner peace does he truly live up to his name and become a peacemaker and only the peacemaker can attain inner peace.

## Inner Conflict and Its Solution

The Society of Friends possesses a great number of spiritual autobiographies or "Journals," as they are usually called, which portray the lives of what might be called "standard Friends." This title is justified because these Journals were at one time read in every Quaker household in order to impress on the hearers the type of life which was the true Quaker norm. Partly through them, the Quaker cultural pattern was passed from one generation to another with remarkable success for nearly two centuries. These Journals sometimes begin with a brief account of a period of early innocence, usually followed by a description of childhood frivolities which the writer looks back upon as a waste of time. After that comes a vivid picture of inner conflict.

The soul is divided, pulled in one direction by the powers of evil and in the opposite direction by the powers of good. For this season of conflict one example will stand for all. The struggle varies in intensity though it does not vary in character. Job Scott (1751-1793) writes a vivid description of his own four years' struggle:

Often in the night and sometimes in the break of day I have returned home from my many meetings grievously condemned, distressed and ashamed, wishing I had not gone into such company and resolving to do so no more. But soon my resolutions failed me and away I went again and again. The Lord followed me close in mercy and often broke in powerfully upon me turning all my mirth into mourning; yet I still got over the holy witness, did despite to the spirit of grace and repaired again and again to the haunts of diversion. Adored forever be the name of the Lord, he forsook me not, but followed me still closer and closer and sounded the alarm louder and louder in my ears. The way was shown me but I would not walk in it. I knew my Lord's will but did it not; mine own I still delighted in. My days I spent in vanity and rebellion; my nights frequently in horror and distress. Many a night I scarce durst enter my chamber or lay me down in bed. . . . I prayed, I cried, I repented, I sinned. God still interrupted my career, disturbed my casual satisfaction and blasted all my joys. In pursuing my course I knew I was pursuing my daily and almost unsupportable distress. I knew myself a prisoner and yet I hugged my chains.

This account is condensed from ten pages of Job Scott's Journal. The passage presents, perhaps in a form more extreme than the average, a common human experience, which is often unrecognized for what it is—an uneasiness due to a pull on the soul by a Power from above which cannot be escaped. It is the experience described by the Psalmist: "Whither shall I go from thy spirit! or whither shall I flee from thy presence?" or by Francis Thompson:

> I fled him down the nights and down the days:
> I fled him down the arches of the years.

Every human soul is pursued by the "hound of heaven," but not every human soul knows what is pursuing him. Job Scott writes of his struggle with an understanding acquired only after the struggle was over. There was no sudden change to a state of peace. He came gradually to realize:

that this inward something which had been thus long and power-fully striving with me was the true and living spirit and power of the eternal God, the very same that strove with the old world, influenced the patriarchs, prophets and apostles and visits, strives with and at seasons more or less influences the hearts of all man-kind. I now saw this the only principle of all true conversion and salvation; that so long as this was resisted and rejected, separa-tion must infallibly remain between God and the soul, but that whenever this is received and in all things thoroughly sub-mitted to, a reconciliation takes place.

This overcoming of the sense of separation was also an ex-perience of the union of his own will with the will of God:

The one thing needful is real union with God, an actual join-ing with him in one spirit. Without this union let a man know what he will, believe, possess and enjoy whatever he may or can, but he is an alien and a wanderer on the earth. Nothing else can ever satisfy his soul or abidingly stay his mind. There is no other possible permanent rest for the sole of his foot. He may drive, toil and bustle about and many may think him in a state of enjoyment, but it is all a delusion. In the midst of all earth's caresses, if he presumes to declare himself happy he does violence to truth and his own feelings and the truly wise are privy to the lie. If he professes religion, goes to meeting, prac-tices the exteriors of devotion and talks much about faith and godliness, it may for a moment quiet his mind and deceive his soul and others but long he cannot rest composed without living union with God.

This "union" was no submergence of Job Scott's individu-ality in some all inclusive Over-Soul, it was rather a willing-ness to submit to the divine requirements whatever they might be, a willingness to take his unique individual part in a life greater than his own.

I gave up very fully and from the heart to serve the Lord in the way of his leadings. I forsook rude and vicious company, withdrew into retirement, attended the meetings of Friends and often sought the Lord and waited upon Him in solemn reverential silence alone for his counsel, direction and preservation.

After this shifting from a human-centered to a divine-centered life, Job Scott became aware of many new requirements, which he must meet if he was to retain the inward peace which he had found. One of these was his appearance in vocal ministry in the meeting for worship. The uneasiness created by holding back disappeared. "I felt," he writes, "the return of peace in my own bosom, as a river of life for a considerable time afterward, sweetly comforting my mind and confirming me in this solemn undertaking." Living up to the divine requirements was no easy matter because new duties were constantly appearing. One of these, for instance, was the requirement to refuse to use the paper currency issued to support the Revolutionary War. Once, when called to undertake a long religious journey, he felt it very hard to leave his wife and children behind and financially dependent on the meeting, but he finally gave way and then he could write, "At this surrender of all things I felt the light of heaven to fill my soul." Such decisions as this would not have been so difficult as they were if the Divine Presence had always been felt. Job Scott frequently underwent periods of aridity which were especially embarrassing when large crowds expecting to hear his ministry attended a meeting which he was visiting. Times of doubt, darkness, failure were, he felt, necessary. "I saw pretty clearly," he writes, "in the midst of my deepest depression that if I should be favored with unremitted tranquility and divine enjoyment I should be in danger of spiritual pride and exaltation." But in spite of these ups and downs the search for, and attainment of, inward peace was a clearly defined process. It consisted of a willingness to obey the will of God in so far as that will could be ascertained.

I have dwelt at length on Job Scott because his life is typical of hundreds of others which are portrayed in the Quaker Journals. An initial conflict is followed by a decision which finally ends it and brings peace. But this decision only begins the long spiritual journey on which there are many difficult hurdles to surmount. The Quakers do not believe, as do some other Christians, that man is born in a state of total depravity and remains in it until he is wholly changed by conversion which transforms him from a state of nature to a completed state of grace. Conversion is the beginning not the end of a process. When inward peace disappears it is a sign that the next stage of growth is at hand and peace can only be reached if that growth takes place. A divine call may come requiring an individual to speak in a meeting. If the call is resisted inward peace disappears. In such a state Martha Routh took to her bed and became so ill that her life was despaired of. David Ferris who resisted for many years was troubled with vivid dreams which were clearly reprimands for his delinquency. Finally, to use the homely figure employed by Samuel Bownas, "the ice is broken," the Friend speaks in meeting, perhaps only to utter a single Bible verse. Profound peace again enters the soul. Hugh Judge of Concord Meeting, Pennsylvania, thus writes of his feelings after his first sermon: "My pen is not able to set forth the awful, solemn quiet, the calm, serene state of mind that I enjoyed for many days, so that it seemed that I had gotten into another world." The same peace comes again and again as each new requirement is met: the adoption of plain dress, the use of thee and thou instead of you, keeping on the hat or some other act considered ill-mannered by the world, undertaking a difficult piece of religious service in a far country when family or business needs might have been thought to demand attention at home.

Most significant in this respect is the curtailment of business when the business has grown to such an extent that it interferes with religious duties. The example of John Woolman is best known, but almost every Journal writer eventually finds it necessary to exercise some restraint in business. Friends acquired a reputation for honesty and industry which frequently resulted in considerable business success. It has been frequently pointed out by historians, Arnold Toynbee among them in his *Study of History,* that material success weakened the spiritual vitality of the Society of Friends. There is truth in this, but in a great many cases Friends found that inward peace could only be attained by reducing their business undertakings. John Barclay speaks for all when he says, "I believe it right to sit loose to this world and the anxieties thereof lest I be incapacitated for performing that service which may be shown to be my duty. I believe it safest for me if in any business it should be one of moderate profit and not involving much attention."[1] But such business was far from being the only distraction which could rob the soul of peace. Rebecca Jones writes: "I have shaken my hands from the gain of schoolkeeping." Catherine Phillips ceases to write poetry; Edward Hicks restrains his inclination to paint pictures; John Rutty reduces time spent in writing books on medicine and William Allen gives up a promising career of scientific research. Such self-surrender is not asceticism; it is an effort to attain integration of personality around a central interest by reducing competing interests. If one's central interest is business, fundamental yearnings of the

[1] This and other examples of curtailment of business are given in *Children of Light,* by H. H. Brinton (New York: The Macmillan Co., 1938), pp. 402-5.

soul would be left unsatisfied. The central interest to which all others are subordinated must be important enough to be worthy of complete, unqualified devotion. The only interest which so qualifies is the religious interest.

## The Philosophical Basis

Inward peace is the result of inward unity, not just a unity of ideas but a unity of the whole person, including those feelings and intuitions which arise out of the deeper areas of the soul which are beyond conscious thought. This inward unity is produced by the divine Light of Truth shining into the Soul from what George Fox called "The hidden unity in the eternal being." The primordial unity of the creative source, if unresisted, produces unity in the individual or the group.

No subtle metaphysic is involved here. We are speaking of a unity of will, not of substance. Since there is only one truth, the parts of the soul, or the individuals in a group, come into unity in so far as they follow the will of their leader. The Light in its wholeness shines into every individual, though that individual's comprehension of it may be very imperfect. In so far as the one Divine Center is approached, so far do the various fragments of an individual person or of a group of persons come into unity.

The process of attaining unity in the individual is similar to the process of attaining unity in the group. A Friends meeting, in making a decision, does not vote, because a vote would emphasize, not remove, an existing division of opinion. A truth must be sought which transcends the fragmentary insights of various individuals or factions. As the discussion proceeds each partial insight supplements every other partial insight until truth emerges and the meeting becomes unified in a single insight. The decision thus arrived at is not intended to be a compromise, though it often is a compromise, but a new creation which no member of the group could have arrived at alone. This method does not always succeed, but it succeeds often enough to justify the theory behind it. It is a method requiring willingness to submerge individual desires and prejudices and to obey the will of God wherever it may lead. Religion in this case is a method whereby, through prayer, worship, and patient waiting, often in silence, the soul may become sensitized to the Light of Truth and willing to submit to it. Only through this attitude of obedience can real inner unity arise either in the individual or in the group. Conflict in the soul arises from refusal to accept the truth. As one Quaker journalist, Stephen Crisp, puts it: "My wisdom and reason were overcome by the truth, I could not therewith withstand it and defended it with the same reason by which I resisted it, and so was yet a stranger to the cross that was to crucify me." Pride, self-will, an exclusive loyalty to one's own fragmentary viewpoint must be crucified if man is to be resurrected into that newness of life in which he is at peace.

## The Place of Self-surrender

Self-surrender of man to God is often misunderstood because of the language used in describing it. The word "surrender" seems to imply an attitude of passivity which is out of tune with the tendency of our present age toward extreme activism. The effort at self-annihilation, accompanied by the expectation that, when all human thought and feeling subsides, God may manifest his redeeming power in the soul is sometimes described as *Quietism*. This word, too, is misleading. It places the emphasis only on the negative side of this religious experience. In Quakerism the negative is not an end in itself but a preparation for the positive. If the lower is quieted it is only that the higher may have opportunity to assert itself. The weeds must be cleared away if the flower is to grow. The human must be still if the divine is to be heard.

In earlier forms of Quaker theology the distinction between the divine and the human is thought of as sharp and definite, in some modern forms divine and human merge as a finger merges into the hand; in either case self-surrender in silent expectant waiting should be the first spiritual exercise, a prerequisite of all others. If divine and human are too closely identified self-surrender becomes meaningless and man remains entangled in the web of his own weaknesses and contradictions. Inward quieting is the negative side of a positive experience. It may even result in intense activity as is illustrated on almost every page of the Quaker Journals. John Woolman while making a dangerous visit to Indians on the frontier writes, "My mind was centered in resignation in which I always found quietness."

No Quaker was more feverishly active than Thomas Shillitoe. He visited "in the love of the Gospel" thousands of drinking houses in Ireland, prisoners and outlaws in various lands, King, Czar and Emperor. Nothing could stop him, though he was by nature a shy and timorous character. The following passage from his Journal discloses the source of his strength:

When I am led to take a view of the accumulated difficulties that I must expect in the prosecution of the work before me, my soul is humbled and bowed within me as into the very dust; whereby my mind at times became sorrowfully charged with an apprehension I should not have strength to proceed agreeably to the expectation I had given my friends, and thereby shamefully expose myself. But divine goodness appeared for my help with the animating assurance, that if I remained willing to become like a cork on the mighty ocean of service, which my great Master should require of me, in the storm and in the calm, free from the lead of human reason, not consulting and conferring with flesh and blood, willing to be wafted hither and thither, as the Spirit of the Lord my God should blow upon me, he would care for me every day and every way; so that there should be no lack of strength to encounter all my difficulties. Here my discouragements vanished.

One of the most powerful preachers of the doctrine of complete resignation as the way to inward peace was Elias Hicks. Expressions like the following abound in his published sermons:

I felt nothing when I came into this meeting nor had I a desire after anything but to center down into abasement and nothingness; and in this situation I remained for a while, till I found something was stirring and rising in my spirit. And this was what I labored after . . . to be empty, to know nothing, to call for nothing, and to desire to do nothing.

It would be useless to multiply such examples. In so far as Quietism means the surrender of the human or self-centered will in order that the divine may become active in and through the human, it is a universal Quaker doctrine. Cut off from the higher God-centered will, the lower self-centered will seeks satisfaction in an area too limited to satisfy it. As a result there is no inward peace. But the remedy is not far off. In the silence of prayer, meditation and worship the soul learns to say "not my will but thine be done." The peace of God floods in and along with the peace of God there also comes sooner or later the call to action without which that peace cannot continue.

George Fox lived a life of tireless activity, but this activity was rooted in inward peace and stillness. Throughout his epistles he calls on Friends to be still. "Stand still in that which is pure after ye see yourselves." "Wait in the Light." "Standing still in the Light within and therein waiting, ye will see your Savior Christ Jesus." "Wait in the Life which will keep you above Words." "Be low and still in the Life and Power." "In the Stillness and Silence of the Power of the Almighty dwell." With this call to stillness there is also a call to that which is cool, and free from the heat of passion and desire. "Dwell in the Cool Sweet Holy Power of God." "Dwell in the endless Power of the Lord—that hath the Wisdom which is sweet and cool and pure." "Be still and cool in thy own mind and spirit."

## The Habitation of Peace

Quaker writers sometimes speak as if there were a calm area in the soul to which one might retire as to a quiet room, well shielded from the outer tumult. Thus Fox writes to some Friends enduring severe persecution, "All in the power of the living God abide in which ye may feel Life, Peace and Rest and an abiding peace, a secret chamber to turn into." And John Woolman writes, "The place of prayer is a precious habitation . . . I saw this habitation to be safe . . . to be inwardly quiet when there were great stirrings and commotions in the world." John Pemberton writes to Susanna Fothergill in 1755 when the French and Indian war was coming on, "Yet there are such that can, in humility and thankfulness say they are favored with a quiet habitation." And John Barclay writes, "Oh it is a sweet thing to get into the calmness, to that spot where all cares, fears, and doubts are swallowed up." This "chamber," "habitation" or "spot" is, in Quaker philosophy, that area of perfect unity and peace which existed before all multiplicity and strife. "Be at peace one with another," writes Fox, "then you will live in the Prince of Peace's peace and in his Kingdom, Dominion and Life in which is unity, which was before Enmity was." "Stand steadfast in the Unchangeable Life and Seed of God which was before all changing and alterings were."

## Getting Atop of Things

That peace can be found within a certain area of the soul is a figure of speech which allocates to space that which is not in space. There is, in Quaker writings, another significant figure based on a space relationship. When Fox describes an encounter with an obstruction of any kind— a person, a doubt, a temptation, a difficult situation—he often ends with the phrase "but I got atop of it." In his epistles he frequently gives advice to others to do likewise: "Keep atop of that which will cumber the mind." "Take heed of being hurried with many thoughts but live in that which goes over them all." "But there is danger and temptation to you of drawing your minds into your business, and clogging them with it: so that ye can hardly do anything to the service of God, but there will be crying my business, my business, and your minds will go into the things and not over the things." "Keep your heads above the waters of the sea in which there is a tempest."

This can be interpreted as meaning that many problems are not soluble on their own level. If there is a conflict of two opposing ideas or feelings and if one simply prevails over the other, eliminating whatever good there may be in the weaker, no real solution is arrived at. Too often the weaker is driven out of sight only to reappear in disguise to continue the conflict. But by achieving a higher, more inclusive experience we can get above the problem, look down on it, and find that it ceases to be a problem. This process is described by the psychologist Jung in more secular terms:

I have often seen individuals who simply outgrew a problem which had destroyed others. This outgrowing revealed itself on further experience to be the raising of the level of consciousness. Some higher or wider interest arose on the person's horizon, and through this widening of his view, the insoluble problem lost its urgency. It was not solved logically in its own terms, but faded out in contrast to a new and stronger life tendency. . . . What on a lower level had led to the wildest conflicts and to emotions full of panic, viewed from the higher level of the personality now seemed like a storm in a valley seen from a high mountain top. This does not mean that the thunderstorm is robbed of its reality; it means that instead of being in it, one is now above it . . . The greatest and most important problems of life . . . can never be solved, but only outgrown.[2]

George Fox in his letter to Cromwell's daughter, Lady Claypole, who was "sick and much troubled in mind" gives advice which fits this doctrine of Jung.

Whatever temptations, distractions, confusions the light doth make manifest and discover, do not look at these temptations, confusions, corruptions; but look at the light, which discovers them, and makes them manifest; and with the same light you may feel over them, to receive power to stand against them. The same Light which lets you see sin and transgression will let you see the covenant of God, which blots out your sin and transgression, which gives victory and dominion over it, and brings into covenant with God. For looking down at sin and corruption and distraction ye are swallowed up in it; but looking at the light which discovers them, ye will see over them. That will give victory; and ye will find grace and strength: there is the first step to peace.

This is quite different from holding that evil is unreal and hence to be ignored. It means that inward conflict is avoided by a kind of pacifist technique which uses no violence on the evil in ourselves. By fixing our attention on the light, the darkness is not only revealed for what it is but also transcended. To use Fox's words we "get atop of it." The dark force of the soul cannot be removed by a direct attack. To fight them is to give them the only real strength which they can possess. They should not be despised or hated. As revealed by the light they must first be accepted for what they are. Then, by allowing the light to shine and so permitting higher forces in the background to emerge and operate, there will arise an interest, a concern, a new life, call it what you will, that will surround and overcome the darkness and center the soul in that which is above it. It is not through

[2] *Secret of the Golden Flower.* (New York: Harcourt Brace & Co., 1931), p. 88.

a struggle to possess the Light but rather by permitting the Light to possess us that inner darkness is overcome. The Quaker Journals do not indicate that this way is always successful. There are many records of long periods of dryness, but sooner or later refreshing showers descend and new life is generated in the soul.

## Inward Peace as a Test of Guidance

Inward peace is both an end and a means. As a means it becomes an evidence of divine approval while lack of it is an evidence that some divine requirement is not being fulfilled. In a Quaker meeting for the business of church government the following expression is frequently heard: "I would feel most easy," or "I would feel comfortable" if such and such an action were carried through or not carried through, indicating that the inward peace of the speaker would be attained only if a certain course were or were not accomplished. Throughout the Quaker Journals we find frequent reference to the absence of inward peace as a sign that some "concern," possibly to undertake a journey "in the love of the gospel," possibly to engage in some effort for social reform, had been laid upon the individual. When that concern has been carried through there is reference to the return of peace. It is not essential that the undertaking be successful for inward peace to result. It is only necessary that the individual feel that he has done all that he is able to do to carry out the requirement. God does not require more than is possible. He only demands that we live up to our capacity. As for consequences, how can a finite mind tell what they in the long course of time may be. History shows many instances of apparent immediate failure resulting in ultimate success. The pacifist, for example, who finds that in joining an army he will have no peace of mind and who for this reason refuses to join may be presented with many excellent arguments which he cannot refute showing him the evil consequences of his refusal, but he knows that his feelings are just as truly organs of knowledge for certain aspects of experience as is reason. If properly sensitized to the perception of moral and religious values, the feelings may be more reliable organs than the intellect. Thought may reveal immediate relative consequences but inspired feeling may go far beyond thought, in some measure revealing the absolute and ultimate.

That inward peace is a test of guidance is, of course, a dangerous doctrine. "Woe unto those who are at ease in Zion." There is a kind of placidity which results from lack of sensitiveness to the needs of others, to callousness and hardness, which shut out the world and its sufferings. Such calm may be genuine for a shellfish but not for a human being. Let him who seeks peace by indifference examine himself closely, he will find that in the depths of his heart there is not really peace. If he attempts to reduce himself to the level of pure sensation he will find it difficult if not impossible to avoid yearning and regret. The peace of callousness is a false peace, a truce concealing hidden conflict.

If inward peace is to be used as a test of guidance two conditions must be honestly met—first the feelings must be sensitized through prayer, worship, meditation or other spiritual exercises, so that they may be trustworthy for ascertaining moral or religious truth.[3] Second, the guidance of the individual must be checked with the guidance of others —the guidance of the group to which he belongs and the guidance of inspired utterances of the past and present. The guidance of the group is not always superior to the guidance of the individual, but it must be taken into account. There is no sure evidence of Divine guidance. The presence or absence

[3] Aesthetic truth could also be included though it is not pertinent to this discussion.

of inward peace, whether in the individual or the group, is a useful test if made under right conditions.

In the days when Friends dealt in a disciplinary way with members who broke with the Quaker standard of behavior, they pointed out to the delinquent individual that the Lord was exerting a pressure on him which was disturbing his peace and that he could remove this pressure by obedience to the Divine Will. David Ferris of Wilmington writes to Robert Pleasants in 1774 regarding his slaves:

> I fear that to hold them in a state of slavery, deprived of their natural right may be a means of depriving thee of thy own freedom, and not only prevent thee from being so serviceable in thy day as otherwise thou might be but a bar in the way of peace here and hereafter . . . I cannot suppose that at this time of the day I need use arguments to convince thee of the evil of slave-keeping. Obedience is what I judge to be wanting; and it is sorrowful to think that people should go on in the way they know to be wrong . . . If the Lord requires thee to set thy slaves free, obey him promptly and leave the result to him, and peace shall be within thy borders.

## The Return to Inwardness

What is called in this essay "The Quaker Doctrine of Inward Peace" is obviously not a doctrine which is unique to the Society of Friends. In its general and essential character it can be found in all the so-called higher religions. What is peculiar to Quakerism is more a matter of emphasis and method than of substance. That a quietistic type of resignation and restraint results, not in retirement to hermitage or cloister, but rather in more intense activity in the world; that a life centered in the peace of God may be lived not only by priest, pastor and religious professional but by merchant, banker, farmer, mother of a large family and all who are in daily contact with a sinful world. Inward peace may be felt in the heart which shares the burden of the world's sufferings—this doctrine has received a peculiar, though by no means an exclusive emphasis, in the Society of Friends.

Only in its method is the Society of Friends unique. The Quaker meeting for worship and the Quaker meeting for business are unique institutions. It is their purpose to expose the soul to the Light from God so that peace is removed if it ought to be removed, or attained if it can be attained. If the soul becomes sensitive, if its vision is widened and deepened so that new areas of life come within its ken, then a new requirement may be laid upon it and peace removed until that requirement is met. If the soul in silence is able to find union with God at the heart of existence, then inward peace is secured and new knowledge and power received. The soul, no longer exhausting its energy in conflict with itself, becomes integrated and unified. Hence arises new power and vision for tasks ahead. This is what Dante expressed by the words, "In His will is our peace."

The examples given in this essay are taken from the seventeenth and eighteenth centuries. This was a time when, among Friends, the inward and outward were comparatively integrated. It was a time of social pioneering in such fields as equality of sexes, races and classes, simplicity of life, peacemaking, prison reform, reform of mental hospitals, abolition of slavery, education. Yet it was also a time of intense inwardness, when the primary emphasis was placed on divine guidance and the search for inward peace. This inwardness increased men's sensitivity to moral evils, and enabled situations to be faced freshly rather than through the obscuring haze of conventional patterns.

Modern Quakerism, affected by the prevailing trends of our time, has lost much of this inwardness. Activity continues to increase. Outward peace is sought as never before but men search less intently for the inward peace which is both source and goal of outward peace.

After a long period of trial we have found that modern scientific skill has brought neither outer nor inner peace. The attention of science has been focused upon the outward, ignoring the fact that the powerful instruments which science has created may be used for good or evil according to the inward state of the men who use them. But even if scientific skill had turned its attention to the inward it would not necessarily ·have brought peace. Applied science may work out methods by which men can control others through advertising or propaganda, but such control can be exerted for good or evil purposes and can therefore create either peace or conflict. In recent years scientific skill has been largely used for conflict, either to promote a militant nationalism or to produce a restless insatiable desire for possessions in order to increase the sale of goods. This is not the road to peace. It is clear evidence that the inner life is evaporating out of our culture, that the soul which held this culture together is vanishing, leaving outer force as a means of providing security and unity.

But in the midst of such disintegration there are now, as there have been in earlier ages, persons and groups who discover or rediscover the sources of peace and unity which have been hinted at in these pages. All men everywhere must come to realize that outer conflict results from inner conflict, that inner conflict can be healed only by that Power divine which descends to men from on high. "Peace I leave with you," said Jesus, "my peace I give unto you: not as the world giveth give I unto you. Let not your heart be troubled, neither let it be afraid."

# 5

# THE SELF TO THE SELF

*Can we become ever more conscious of the selves within our self . . . the deep, constant self; the bright, acceptable, recognized self and the dark, unadapted, unknown brother; the body and the soul, the heart and the mind; "that of God within" which must surely have somewhere a counterpart— that of the Devil?*

DORA WILLSON

Dora Willson's work combines the insights of a person born in England and educated in Switzerland, and trained at the University of Geneva both in psychology and in teaching. She has been a social worker in Switzerland and a research worker in psychology in Egypt. She has worked in American Friends Service Committee projects and in high schools in Denmark and in the United States. As lecturer at Pendle Hill, she has developed special techniques for group study and discussion of the gospels; as counselor to students she has encouraged the use of the tools of psychology on emotional and spiritual problems. Dora Willson's two Pendle Hill pamphlets, *The Totalitarian Claim of the Gospels*, 1939, and *The Self to the Self*, 1947, joint products of a single search, have been brought together specially for this collection.

There was once a man, we are told, who being asked his name, answered "Legion." That is every man's name. Most of us realize its appropriateness only intermittently and usually feel ourselves to be "single"—which is perhaps just as well. Nevertheless life seems to insist, in one way or another, that we gain some awareness of our various selves— or aspects of our personality, or whatever we wish to call the "others" who, with "me," make up the "legion." A conscious effort. Many more people go through life unaware that one of the main causes of the ever-recurring complications besetting them is the inadequacy or the breakdown of their inner relationships. We dwell usually in the self's front parlor, kept neat and ready for visitors, but neglect our back rooms and our cellars. Can we be wise householders and not make use of all our house? Can we become ever more conscious of the selves within our self; the obvious, rational, adult self; the hidden, irrational, childish self; the shifting, changing, surface self; the deep, constant self; the bright, acceptable, recognized self and the dark, unadapted, unknown brother; the body and the soul, the heart and the mind; "that of God within" which must surely have somewhere a counterpart—that of the Devil?

Yes, man has always said that it *is* possible to encompass this unending variety in some sort of relationship, not only possible, but necessary for life. From the dawn of history we can trace man's efforts in this direction and see how he found in religion, as its very name indicates, that which *ties together* what is separate into a functioning whole. So we are not surprised that all religions and most philosophies insist on self-awareness as a basic requirement, from the "know thyself" of Socrates to the less familiar, noncanonical saying of Jesus, "Strive . . . to know yourself, and ye shall be aware that ye are the sons of the almighty Father; and ye shall know that ye are in the city of God and ye are the city." And we find many clear passages on this point in the writings of early Friends. Isaac Penington writes,

O my Friend! mind this precious Truth inwardly, this precious grace inwardly, the precious life inwardly, the precious light inwardly, the precious power inwardly, the inward word of life, the inward voice of the Shepherd in the heart, the inward seed, the inward salt, the inward leaven, the inward pearl. . . . Distinguish between words *without* concerning the thing, and the thing itself *within*; and wait and labour, then, to know, understand, and be guided by, the motives, leadings, drawings, teachings, quickenings, etc. of the thing itself within.

There seem to be two main questions which need to be deeply lodged and distinctly stated: Of what nature should our relation to ourself be? How establish and maintain and develop it?

## How Self Relates to Self

Jesus said that the way of life was to follow the two great commandments: "You shall love the Lord your God with all your heart, and with all your soul, and with all your mind, and with all your strength," and "You shall love your neighbor as yourself." Why has this last clause, the third relationship, that of the self to the self, been so consistently ignored or even contradicted? Ignoring it may be more dangerous than we think. Jesus' answer to the scribe astounds one by its unassailability—not pushing a man off in the vague regions of God off the earth—but holding him right here, confronted by fellow human beings. This commandment is planted right down upon human relationships, compassed amazingly—without a code, not a word of code—in "as thyself." The second half of the commandment is no mean perception; it is the discovery that in human relationship you don't need to read the books, just read yourself.

Straightforward as this is, it is not simple to apply. So beset with misleading bypaths is the way to self-knowledge and self-love that many, realizing the dangers, have tried to avoid it altogether. In so doing, they have missed the way to love of others, for the two "ways" are in reality one, as the second commandment states clearly. Often they are separated. For Calvin, love of self is a "pest," love of others a virtue. Sinful man is but a worm; he should find nothing lovable about himself; that would be selfishness, one of the greatest of sins. But observe how this position, so plausible, so apparently noble and disinterested, has a sterilizing effect upon love of others. Love becomes a duty, a virtue to be practiced *because* it is a virtue, instead of being the ever-renewed outflowing result of a creative inner relationship. From this static altruism it is but a step to the neglect or contradiction of the second commandment as a whole. And in fact we find Calvin at one point saying, "For what the schoolmen advance concerning the priority of charity to faith and hope, is a mere reverie of a distempered imagination. . . ." We may remember also the Puritans' distrustful attitude towards all men. Since man was essentially evil, how could it be expected that he be lovable? It is instructive to remember the saints who came inductively to the same evaluation of the sinfulness of man, but knew nevertheless that it is possible to "love him even under a blight," to love him even *as* a sinner, without admiring him, because God himself loves man.

When the pendulum swung from Calvinlike self-abasement, it swung too far. The necessity of selfishness, self-love, self-regard was advocated indiscriminately, and love of others was held up as weakness. Nietzsche, whose name comes inevitably to mind, had glimpses of deeper understanding, however. The love of neighbors which he condemns is one which is rooted in a wrong attitude toward oneself; a right relation to oneself would lead to a right relation with others. "Your neighbor love is your bad love for yourselves," he says in *Thus Spake Zarathustra*. "You flee into your neighbors from yourselves and would fain make a virtue thereof. But I fathom your unselfishness. . . . You cannot stand yourselves and you do not love yourselves sufficiently."

When we look at modern man, baffled by the contradictions of his guides, we see that the false opposition between love of self and love of others is still part of his daily pattern. True, our "enlightened," liberal thinking has dropped the emphasis on the utter worthlessness of man, but the optimism is usually rooted in shallow ground and the confusion worse than ever, for while altruism is taught in school and church and home, and even in popular literature and the movies, an open naïve respect is paid to self-advancement and a crude and unashamed concern for self alone is recommended as the means of assuring the "good of the whole."

It is not necessary here to trace in detail the consequences for the individual and for society of the neglect of the pivotal clause in the principle, "love thy neighbor *as thyself.*" It may be worth while, however, to glance at the widely accepted interpretations of love of self as selfishness, and of love of others as unselfishness. It is not to be wondered at if we hardly know what true love is, for the false forms of love are numerous. Much of literature has been occupied with depicting them. One terrifying example is found in Stephen Vincent Benét's *John Brown's Body.* Lucy, in front of her mirror, talks to herself:

> "Honey, I love you," she whispers, "I love you, honey.
> Nobody loves you like I do, do they, sugar?
> Nobody knows but Lucy how sweet you are.
> You mustn't get married, honey. You mustn't leave me."

In this description, as in many others, we can see how subtly imitative is the false article. But true love and its imitations spring from different sources and it is at their point of origin that we may most easily distinguish them from each other. True love grows out of a positive, affirmative attitude towards life and all its potentialities. False forms of love grow out of dislike, distrust, and the fear and insecurity which follow. They are attempts at bolstering up, at defending a threatened citadel, and usually the attacks are imagined as coming from without, when the enemy is within and his position strengthened, therefore, by the mistaken defense. Thus also true unselfishness and readiness to sacrifice one's self grow out of a generalized state of affirmation of life and its values. The sacrifice is then not an end in itself, a supreme virtue, but a means, the only appropriate and adequate means on occasion, to affirm and express one's loyalty to the values prized. False unselfishness, on the contrary, is rooted in a deep distrust of and dislike for the self—so deep as to be unrecognized, usually. The terrible insecurity which results may lead to a grasping selfishness, but also often, to the passionate throwing away of oneself into a greater whole where security may be expected.

This is the seeming unselfishness which Nietzsche recognized, which may be a result of the self having been patterned from childhood up on all the models presented by family and society. There may even be no conflict because there is no consciousness of a self which is not thus patterned. This adaptation may last until death and apparently be successful, but we know that someone sometime will have to solve the unsolved problems. "For I the Lord thy God am a jealous God, and visit the sins of the fathers upon the children unto the third and fourth generation."

I would like here to quote Erich Fromm, who speaks from inside experience of the use Nazism made of this deep-rooted urge to self-sacrifice:

The authoritarian propaganda uses the argument that the individual of the democratic state is *selfish* and that he should become unselfish and socially minded. . . . The appeal for unselfishness is the weapon to make the average individual still more ready to submit or to renounce. The criticism of democratic society should not be that people are too selfish; this is true but it is only a consequence of something else. What democracy has not succeeded in is to make the individual love himself; that is, to have a deep sense of affirmation for his individual self, with all his . . . potentialities. . . . The readiness for submission, the pervert *courage* which is attracted by the image of war and self-annihilation, is only possible on the basis of a—largely unconscious—desperation, stifled by martial songs and shouts for the Fuhrer. The individual who has ceased to love himself is ready to die as well as to kill. The problem of our culture, if it is not to become a fascist one, is not that there is too much selfishness but that there is no self-love.[1]

One further point. True love knows no limits as to its objects. It cannot possibly attach itself, for instance, to the self and in so doing turn one from proper concern for others. Nor on the other hand can it be directed towards others and require that one have no regard for oneself. No, its all-inclusiveness is its hallmark, its distinguishing characteristic by which we may infallibly recognize it.

This may be easier to see in the case of the contrary relationship, hate. I do not mean hate as a healthy specific reaction to an attack on something valued and positively affirmed. I mean that poisonous hate which is a condition of character, a fundamental, dormant, indiscriminate hatred, growing out of frustration and negativism, which may be stirred into action either by objects outside the self or by the self itself. This chronic basic state of latent hostility is one of the major problems of our day. Few of us are conscious of it in ourselves, at most we perceive its reflection—indifference to others. The majority are not even aware of that, for we are socially well-adapted, we *like* people in a promiscuous, neutral way, and are in a state of suspended relationship, as it were, with ourselves. But we cannot help revealing our inner condition. As individuals we have feelings of inferiority or an exaggerated tendency to be self-critical, and especially do we betray ourselves in our treatment of ourselves as slaves, giving to our conscience the false role of inward mouthpiece of external authority. And as members of groups or nations,

[1] Erich Fromm, *Man for Himself, An Inquiry into the Psychology of Ethics* (New York: Rinehart & Co., 1947).

we let our inner hostility appear even more unmistakably, pooling it in the tragic anonymous world-wide destructiveness of our age.

## The Way to Right Relatedness

How do we come to a true creative love of self? Most of us come, some time or other, to the place where we must deliberately set out to become acquainted with ourself, a basic requirement obviously, yet often a neglected one. We have to catch ourself off guard.

Listening to ourself, to the ever-flowing inner conversation we hold with ourself, is sometimes astonishingly revealing. At first it may be an effort even to hear this monologue, but if we patiently pay attention, as to a child who is learning to speak, it will emerge more and more clearly. Then we can begin to sense something of the hopes and fears, the loves and hates that live under the surface, and we can experiment with following out some of those indications.

Here are the observations of a woman who tried this device for the first time when she was a mature person:

I have been helped during these last few years to sense out the difference between the self and the Self, and to learn to watch and wait and feel in order to come as close as possible to what the Self wants the self to do. I got my first big clue when it was suggested to me that I follow for a week what I *wanted* to do—not what I thought I was supposed to do. The plan seemed too good to be true at first, and my old self felt I *must* be on the wrong path when I did what I really wanted to do—but I found that though I, at the time, seemed to have to choose *not* to do what my husband or immediate friends around wanted of me—that when I followed the spontaneous urge, I actually during a time of days or weeks *did* achieve also what "they" wanted of me—but "their wanting" had to be removed as a motive, or I would be punctilious as a sense of duty and then inwardly or outerly hit out at "them" or at some other puppets outer or inner.

Observing our spontaneous reactions, especially our emotional reactions, to persons and events, may also help us discover ourselves. On occasion it is valuable to write down these reactions, in the form of conversation, for instance, or to express them in other ways, such as painting and dancing.

It should be noted that it may be necessary to cultivate a respect for our potentialities, to trust our inner self before we can even enter into any kind of working agreement with it. The following paragraphs were written by the woman quoted above:

To me the Self is the Lord in the statement, "The Fear of the Lord is the Beginning of Wisdom," in the sense that we should "fear" and treat with awe the life force in us, the God in us. Otherwise we are people trying to keep new wine in old bottles (i.e. a god in a physical body that doesn't accept that it houses a god). Then the god springs out like the geni from the bottle, driven by compulsions or tantrums or restlessness—all signs that the god can't be bottled up.

This inner Self may call my bluff by reacting on my blood and heart-beat or some other part of me until I admit, "Yes, I have concealed my true Self in order to convince not only others but even myself that I was being good, dutiful, loving, cooperative. All right then, you and I can't live in the same physical house—one of us has to give in—and naturally the Self has to win for me to survive."

This elementary process of getting acquainted with ourself implies a certain amount of objectivity, a readiness to see and acknowledge the reality of elements usually hidden and not always agreeable to face. But all religions and all men of insight, and we ourselves when we are free or desperate enough to be honest, know that the accepting and assimilating of these hidden elements is a necessity. We are dual in nature and our task and our glory is to balance the opposites in ourself, to hold them in an ever-renewed polarity of creative tension. Some of the early followers of Jesus were so convinced of this primary duty of reconciling the opposites within the self that they interpreted much of his teaching to apply to this inner problem. Thus, in the second century A.D. we have the Gnostics rewording Matthew 5:23-25 as follows:

If therefore thou art offering thy gift at the altar, and there rememberest that thou hast aught against thyself, leave there thy gift before the altar and go thy way; first be reconciled to thyself and then come and offer thy gift. Agree with thyself quickly, whilst thou art in the way with thyself; lest haply thou deliverest thyself to the judge. . . .

Increasing freedom from fear of inferiority is one of the earliest consequences of the growing ability to see and assimilate the less known and less desirable elements of ourself. This is not "making a pact of friendship" with evil: Jesus did not condone evil but he also did not condemn the sinner, he accepted him. In the noble and practical words of Francis de Sales:

Be patient with everyone, but above all, with yourself. I mean, do not be disheartened by your imperfections, but always rise up with fresh courage. I am glad you make a fresh beginning daily; there is no other means of attaining the spiritual life than by continually beginning again, and never thinking that we have done enough. How are we to be patient in bearing with our neighbor's faults, if we are impatient in bearing our own? He who is fretted by his own failings will not correct them; all profitable correction comes from a calm, peaceful mind.

To sum up this process of finding and assimilating the hidden self, I will quote a passage in one of George Fox's letters which describes it with amazing insight and refreshing imagery:

And so, the Lord God Almighty keep you in his power and wisdom and by it bind the unruly; and when ye have bound them, then ye may speak to them, and by it to fetter them; then ye may catch them, when ye will, when they are fettered.

And get the yoke upon the wild heifer; then will ye save yourselves from a push. . . . And see that ye keep the bit in the wild
horse's mouth, whereby his head may be held down. And how-
soever see that he be bridled, then with the Power he will be
ordered, though he snuffs and snorts, the bridle being kept in
his mouth, he is held down by it. . . . And when this is done,
being kept in the Power ye will know him that rides meekly
upon the foal of the ass . . . to Jerusalem, the highest place of
worship. . . .

Deliberate, rational devices, while necessary to start most
of us off on our voyage of discovery, will not lead us all the
way or indeed perhaps very far toward self-knowledge and
self-understanding and self-love. Other less logical, less
grown-up procedures must be adopted. Two may be suggested: the one a somewhat specialized use of silence, the
other, the deliberate use of *symbols*.

As we all know, messages come in various ways during
times of quiet. Words may be heard inwardly, and sometimes
will seem unintelligible. But we should pay attention to them
and hold them in our mind and examine them and sift them
later. For some to whom music is meaningful, a song or a
fragment of melody may sing itself in the silence, remembered or unknown. Or an image may arise. One such vision,
full of meaning for the one to whom it came, was of a great
river—the river of life—with many people struggling or
drifting in it as they were swept along. A few on the banks
called to those in the water and now and then, with pain
and effort, some climbed onto the shore into conscious,
responsible living.

We may find it worth while to write down any such over-
flowings from the unlimited and uncharted deeps which surround us. Even if reflection does not reveal at once any
logical meaning, let us file away these secret messages, those
at least that carry with them some emotional quality that
makes them significant. Later, life may offer us the code.

Symbols have been found of help by mankind universally

and throughout the ages in tapping depths far below the level of words. This generation is realizing more and more that it needs to turn to the rich heritage that lies at hand. For instance there is the symbol of the garden, the enclosed garden with its four gates and its cruciform paths, and, where they intersect, always water, a spring or a fountain or a well. Or we can take the circle or the cross, one of humanity's most precious symbols, the individual ever crucified on the opposites of human nature. But it is better still for each to find and use his own symbols and in so doing come to see the value of the outward and visible form: the candle, the flower, the corner of desk or mantelpiece where our secret altar may take shape. As a matter of fact, the question is not whether we will make use of symbols or not. There is a choice between using them consciously and appropriately and letting them sway and determine us without control on our part. The rationalist at one extreme, the unconscious religionist at the other, are always in danger of being overwhelmed by some symbol which is imposed or imposes itself upon them. To ignore the tremendous role which symbols play for good or evil in every one's life means at the least turning from a very direct way of relating our self to our deepest self. A trusting, imaginative use of the symbols that are to be found naturally as soon as we look around questingly for them, may in unpredictable measure enrich and enliven our relation to ourself, and therefore our relation to others. Those of us priviliged to have contact with young children will be encouraged by their delighted and uninhibited response. "Except ye become as little children . . ." may mean the ability to see through the transparent envelope of fact the shining symbol of the inexpressible.

## Jesus and the Way

These are methods but the methods are the outgrowth of a Way, a goal so single and complete that it takes the self

and remakes it. Anyone who has the privilege of coming
to the Gospels with a mind undulled by familiarity is impressed at once with the singleness of aim shown by Jesus.
That this characteristic should emerge as sharply as it does,
in spite of the inevitable distortion of the records, is an
added testimony to its power. The brief period of Jesus'
public activity was lived entirely under the compulsion of
one single motive—to make clear to men the way to full
abundant life which he had found. With an equally single
loyalty, he held to the method he had chosen to reach his
objective. This method was teaching. He lived as an itiner-
ant teacher and he centered his teaching on that which was
for him essential: the process, the means by which men might
attain fullness of life. Nowhere in these Gospels do we find
any extensive descriptions of objectives, results, ends. Often
Jesus gives examples of how that person will function in
daily life who has found and followed the Way. But there is
little trace of that which is frequent in the writings of many
mystics: vivid accounts of states of bliss beyond the reach of
human understanding. Such terms as "life," "kingdom of
God," are used by Jesus to describe the wholly satisfactory
results of the right process—these are vague, general terms
to which anyone, from the most highly developed to the
simplest, can give content. In the same way, and with the
same uncompromising absolutism, Jesus speaks of the results of the wrong process as "destruction."

This absolutism of Jesus, so evidently an integral part of
his personality and so clearly expressed in his course of action, is reflected in his teaching on the Way to life. Or perhaps it would be more exact to say that the Way which led
him to life is of such a nature that those who follow it become absolutists. However that may be, the clarity of his
own understanding of that which lay behind his own attainment of life must have been exceptional. Nothing is more

difficult to state lucidly than the steps, often half or wholly unconscious, which lead to spiritual results. Nothing is more difficult to answer than the question, "What must I do to be saved?"

It would seem as though Jesus considered this the question most worthy of answer. We find teaching on the Way scattered throughout the Gospels, evidence that time and again he must have returned to it, using different wording, parables, analogies, varied figures of speech, in his eagerness to make men understand.

Is the process so complicated then, so hard to comprehend? That would not seem to have been Jesus' view; on the contrary, it appeared to him as a Way open to anyone. Of all the prerequisites usually set forth by religious teachers, Jesus assumes one only: moral earnestness, a deep desire for life. That slender foothold is all that man needs, it would seem, to start on the Way. No preliminary beliefs in anything or anyone, beyond that general innate belief in life and in the validity of wanting it for one's self. No intellectual grasp of the nature of God, man or the universe. No conviction of personal sin to be washed clean by the self-sacrifice of another. A singular simplicity of conception. None should draw back, saying he lacks intellectual ability or spiritual insight. "Ho, everyone that thirsteth . . ."

But this does not imply an easy process. Elsewhere Jesus speaks of the narrow gate and the straitened way which few find. If on the one hand no special qualifications of mind or spirit are indispensable, and yet on the other, few are those who find the Way, it must be because something is required other than reasoning or spiritual exercises, something apparently more arduous, more exacting. As Jesus makes abundantly clear, what is required is action, action of such a fundamental nature that one might call it *the* action, the supreme and decisive act by which man gains a new life, enters into a new world. No wonder the image of birth imposes itself: as truly creative as the act that brings forth a living child into the physical world is that act whereby man emerges into fullness of life.

One of the first things to be noticed in Jesus' teaching about the Way is that others, by following it, become his brethren. "Whosoever shall do the will of God, the same is my brother, and sister, and mother." The results which he had attained are attainable by others. It is suggestive to consider the implications of this as to the method Jesus himself had followed. This necessary and decisive step had been taken by him. It is out of his own experience that he describes it. He speaks with an authority different from that of the scribes. It is authority that rests within, in that which he has lived. It is the kind of authority which we respect, comparable to that of the genuine scientist who has carefully followed the specifications for his experiments and whose statements are based on facts he has himself established. Jesus affirms again and again that the results are confidently to be expected: one becomes his brother or sister; one enters the kingdom; the merchant obtains the pearl of great price; life is saved. This quietly triumphant conviction is unmistakable. Unmistakable too are the results seen in Jesus: the objectivity with which he regards himself, the receptive attitude toward all who come to him, even, it would seem, toward inquirers from the groups most likely to be hostile to him, the Pharisees and the scribes; and above all the utter freedom with which he moves through life and meets success and apparent disaster. This freedom is rooted in a deep sense of security. "Be not afraid of them which kill the body," he said to his friends. He was not afraid: nor had he cause to fear "him, which after he hath killed hath power to cast into hell." His was the supremely strengthening experience of knowing himself to be well-pleasing to God. The relationship he had achieved with God convinced him of a sustaining and ever watchful love which banished fear. The Way may be such that few find it, but when seen clearly and followed, it leads infallibly to life. Jesus may have hoped that more would find it if it were described in terms both practical and precise. He used all his superb gifts of insight and expression to tell men what this decisive act is. Two things he makes clear: (1) it involves the whole personality; (2) it is directed toward the Totality which he calls God.

Unlike the scientist who, in carrying out his experiments, always reserves those areas of his self that do not lie within their scope, the man who enters upon this vital experiment must throw in his whole self. This would seem to be the one essential condition for success. Jesus states it in a number of different ways: the parables of the treasure and of the pearl show us men who are obliged to give all they have in exchange for that one thing which they want. The rich ruler who has obeyed the ethical code of his day in its entirety but without feeling that he has gained eternal life, has made one reservation; when this is pointed out to him, he is unwilling to give it up and goes away sorrowful. The lawyer knows the way to eternal life. He quotes a formulation from his own Scriptures which Jesus accepts as adequate, adding only that it must be put into effect. It is a statement of a double relationship, the first between man and God, the second between man and man, and the first is of such a nature that man's whole self is absorbed in it. And in that pregnant saying which has been called the most profound that has ever passed the lips of man, "Whosoever shall seek to gain his life shall lose it: but whosoever shall lose his life shall preserve it," Jesus states the Way in terms of the true relation of self to Self.

Sayings such as these, while they make obvious the costliness of the experiment, do not yield their full meaning at a glance. It would be strange if they did. But it is not abstract reasoning that is needed to understand them. Rather it is that intense scrutiny, made urgent by deep personal concern, which any man who is in earnest about his life will give to possible methods of attaining its fulfillment. Everything would seem to turn upon the meaning of that which has to be given by the individual. What is this "all"? Where lie the boundaries of the Self? Does one ever reach the point where one may say: Nothing is now held back? On the possibility of giving an intelligible answer to such questions as these may depend the whole future of man.

Here confused thinking is prevalent. The Way is sometimes restated in terms of ethical conduct, as if one could attain goodness bit by bit and thus reach life. In other words, results are taken for causes: the visible manifestations of the process are thought to be the process itself and men try to reach the goal by forcing themselves to a mechanical repetition of what can only be spontaneous fruits. Nothing is more baffling than such misconceptions, nor more completely calculated to discourage. Jesus is too clear-minded ever to talk of perfectionism of conduct as the Way. We may consider that he is a perfectionist, but in an utterly different field. As long as we are concerned with good conduct, we are enmeshed in the specific, in details, in parts and fragments of ourselves.

But the crux of the matter, as we saw, is that the totality of the individual has to be committed to this experiment. Can we get the totality by listing the parts, beginning for instance with the more obvious external possessions, and passing to one's affections, desires, ambitions, and so on? The piecemeal process is apparently endless. Jesus evidently meant something else, for his descriptions are always of processes that come to completion, that are followed by the desired outcomes. Is there then some other way of encompassing the self? Instead of working inward from the periphery, so to speak, is it possible to make a direct drive for that which may be central? Is there a point beyond which there would be no need to go, for having reached it one is at the very core of being and if that be handed over, the whole self, good and bad, is also handed over? Is that the point within one's self where decisions are made?

If one could envisage the complete abandonment of one's self to another human being, that would be the ultimate surrender: *You* choose, *you* decide between right and wrong. *I* do what *you* decide. We feel instinctively how utterly wrong it would be if this agreement were entered into between human beings. It is equally tragic for any institution to make any such claims upon men, as we see at once if we use the simple criterion of Jesus, "By their fruits ye shall know them," and trace through history the often appalling results of such attempts. Jesus makes it very clear that man can safely hand over his self-direction only to that which is absolute, all-inclusive, without limit. Jesus uses the word God. Not the specific good recognized as such, nor the totality of those ideals by which mankind tries to guide its conduct and which all too often cripple rather than help, not a code of ethics, however venerable, not even the so-called Golden Rule. These are all partial interpretations, caught in the net of space and time, subject to change with our changing conditions. Only the Totality, beyond the farthest reach of our knowing and of our imagining, is a sufficient object for the total devotion that is required.

In every individual there is a point where the Totality touches the self and the self is enabled to transcend its own limits. Many and beautiful are the expressions men have used to try to describe this: they have called this point of fusion the light which lighteth every man, the seed, that of God within. If these seem too poetic, let us simply look steadfastly within our self at that ineradicable sense of right and wrong which is in every man, in the plainest of language, which is as inadequate as the most elaborate. Where we may look, where we *must* look to make a start is at that point where we decide our conduct. When that sense is blunted by deliberate misuse, the unforgiveable sin against the Holy Spirit is committed; as Jesus declares in one of his most categorical sayings, the sin from which, in the very nature of the case, there is no redress. On the other hand, contact is at once established with the Whole when man takes as sincere a decision as he knows how to make, to be loyal to the directions which come to him, however imperfectly.

Even when the decision is taken at a very humble level, without reference to religious beliefs, the radical act of abdication to the unspecified good bears fruit. Though repeated failures of realization follow immediately, the self has been born into a new life of freedom and potency, and persistent renewal of the pledge brings increase of strength. There may never be ecstasies or visions, there may never be even the sense of Presence, but Jesus seems to take for granted that there will be heightened moral sensitivity and power and sureness in living unknown to those who simply strive to lead good lives. No infallible assurance as to what is right in every specific occasion is promised: indeed Jesus himself was uncertain as to the content of the will of God for him at the very eve of his death, and the account of Gethsemane shows how in the severest crisis that will is sought—by holding the self in absolute availability. In fact, it would seem rather as if life presents dilemmas of increasing difficulty as fineness of discrimination grows. But one thing is gained: when the right is seen, there need be no struggle to force oneself to do it. Not that perfect action will inevitably result. Jesus does not seem to consider perfectionism of action as part of the indispensable condition for entrance into life. Failure we know we must expect here. The indispensable condition is that, in spite of failure, we renew the initial commitment: all of my self to the Whole—known, unknown, unknowable; full control to that which is mediated to me through the in-dwelling sense of right, cost what it may; walls pulled down, unimpeded ingress offered to God. The regnancy of God, the kingdom of God: that is what Jesus called the result of that act; my self-direction unreservedly handed over, my personal self transcended, a new self released into power and life.

The dangers of pulling out of the river of life onto the shore of increasing awareness are many and subtle. A certain loneliness is one result, however vital the sense of growing relationships. And the risks of taking a false path are constant. And so it is good for us to remind ourself frequently that we are not the creators of our relationship with ourself, we do not make it, we prepare the way only, clear the ground, open the gates. Now we must learn the lesson of waiting and respecting life's tempo, the tempo of life's coming:

The Kingdom of God is like a man who sows the seed in the ground. He sleeps by night and rises by day, while the seed springs up and grows—he knows not how. The earth bears crops of itself: first the blade, then the head, then the full grown grain.

Whenever we do our part and our part alone in this des-perate venture, then comes the reward. Then perchance it happens that we, rightly related to ourselves, know ourselves rightly related to all—and, greeting ourselves in true love, we find we hold the hand of our fellow man and that the hand of God holds both of ours.

# 6

# COMMUNITY AND WORSHIP

*It is good to work. It is still better that our work should lead up to letting God work. It is good to pray. It is still better to be prayed in. . . . We may let God work when we yield to the reknitting of the worshipping community itself as the members are drawn nearer to the center and to each other.*

DOUGLAS V. STEERE

One of the leaders of the Society of Friends, Douglas V. Steere is a teacher who has combined wide-ranging intellectual discipline with insight into inward religion. A student of agriculture at Michigan, he changed to the study of philosophy at Harvard. Later at Oxford he became interested in the mysticism of Von Hügel and in the principles and practices of the Society of Friends. His continuing pursuit of the field of inward religion has led him constantly into areas of practice as well as thought: speaking throughout the country, encouraging work camps, developing fellowship groups, leading the retreat movement and traveling in Germany and Scandinavia for the American Friends Service Committee. Douglas Steere is Thomas Wistar Brown Professor of Philosophy at Haverford and author of *On Beginning from Within, Time to Spare, Doors Into Life,* and other books. His essay on community first appeared in 1940.

Some years ago when the Florida authorities asked the man who tried to assassinate Franklin D. Roosevelt whether he belonged to a church, he replied, "No, no, I belong to nothing. I belong only to myself, and I suffer."

These pitiful words express the pain in the hearts of a

vast number of modern men and women: they belong only to themselves, and they suffer. Often enough they are nominal members of a church, a family, or some other organization; yet they have never experienced genuine participation in a religious community which, by dispossessing them of themselves, could free them to belong to life.

Where can these people find a community of men and women and children, of all ages and of many different callings, who are under active treatment by a spirit that is releasing them from themselves, and how can they come into direct contact both with the releasing agent Himself and with the health-giving atmosphere of such a company?

The kind of religious communion that rests content with gathering people for public worship once a week and for an occasional public lecture or social affair might seem sufficient in periods when society is closely knit and when it is easy, as Gerald Heard has suggested, to "mistake comfort for civilization"; but today, when the currents of secular life have weakened the natural bonds and when world events threaten to dissolve them still further, something more elemental becomes imperative if we are to be strong enough to live in our time without succumbing to its demonic forces.

Where, then, can seeking men and women find a community in which meditation, worship, religious education of children, common undertakings and adventurous experiments, common festivals, and spiritual therapy are all going on, not as part of an expensive organized professional program, but as part of the informal natural life of a close religious fellowship?

Let us examine at random a few of the significant groups that both in our own day and in the past have responded to the common yearning for such an intimate spiritual community.

### Therapeutic Groups

Because the church has not adequately supplied this need for intimate fellowship, psychotherapists today are seeking to meet it by setting up institutions in which teachers of gymnastics and of techniques for relaxation, spiritual directors, and handicraft teachers, together with those who are suffering from nervous tensions, all lodge and work and play and study together as an organic interdependent community. For the limited clientele who can afford such an experience, results are being accomplished which surpass anything that has been achieved by the use of private therapy. It is as though in this island community, long overdue readjustments of patterns of living can be undertaken and new standards of value formed, in a way that is impossible when the metallic attractions of a chaotic outer life deflect the needle of the inward compass.

The limited scope of this exclusive community is all too soon revealed, however, when the participant recovers and returns to his former routine of life. He has been given no adequate philosophy to take with him, and his deepest hunger has been neither recognized nor fed.

Gerald Heard has been sensitive to this need for centers of close community life. Perhaps the most valuable sections of his book, *Pain, Sex, and Time,* are devoted to describing the community that will heal the "fissured, distracted, contemporary man." Heard puts forward the proposal for self-supporting communities including in their program individual and corporate meditation, manual work, and group therapy. Each of these communities would be built around and inspired by a master or masters who have themselves found the way to inner health and who have developed inner maturity, so that there is released through them an unmistakable and almost irresistible spiritual power. These men or women would act as spiritual guides for the other members, who would come there for help in removing "the kinks and strangulations" in their inner lives and in recovering their spiritual health in order to return to the world again. "They would be the modern and progressive form of Franciscan tertiaries."

There must be, however, no concealing of the fact that Gerald Heard expects his real results from the masters or "primaries" or "doctors."

When we consider the enormous influence which has always been exercised by men who had no power but their terrible integrity—how Herod feared the Baptist, how Ivan the Terrible dreaded the fakir monk who day by day denounced him in the Red Square of Moscow, how Cromwell was disturbed by Fox, how the Caliph listened to Francis—there can be no historical doubt that the dictator type, the demonic man, is if anything more vulnerable to the charges of the fearless mystic than is the average sensual man. . . . This neo-doctor having no property and no executive power, would be the incarnate conscience of mankind, the inspired actual sanction of conduct which can lead humanity out of its impasse.

There is a flavor of Hinduism and of Zen Buddhism about both the character and the objective of Heard's proposals that will put off most of his critical readers, yet there are many elements in his proposals that point the way to the fellowship, to the spiritually integrated community which we need.

### The Monastic Community

In the monastic life of an order such as the Benedictines, where manual labor, intellectual studies, and devotional exercises supply the needs of body, mind, and spirit, there is a fertile organic community. Here, with the life of the spirit at the center, some of the freest human beings in history were nurtured and kept in a creative balance. Benedict and

Bernard of Clairvaux are only two of a great company. Under the auspices of the Benedictine fellowship a thousand years of western civilization and learning were held together. The only successful attempt in the West to approach the ideal of "To each according to his need, from each according to his ability" was here carried out.

Yet the exclusive nature of this community, its unwillingness to embrace the family, and its consequent reliance upon the outside world for novices, limit the scope of its usefulness. Its rigid medievalism, moreover, precludes the possibility of its becoming the pattern of the new religious community that we need.

### The Third Order of the Franciscans

In 1220 Francis of Assisi was preaching up and down Italy. Wherever he went, he stirred a new sense of repentance and a longing to respond to the love of God, not only in the young and the unmarried, but also in many who carried the responsibilities of a family and of earning a livelihood. These cried out for a rule of life wherein they too might give their all to God. In response to this demand Francis of Assisi set up the Brothers and Sisters of Penance, commonly known as the Third Order of Franciscans, in contrast to the first order of Friars Minor, who were monks, and the second order of Poor Claires, who were nuns. The Third Order was a lay society of men and women who lived a normal life in the world, took all the responsibilities of self-support, vocation, marriage, bearing and rearing of children, and yet resolved to live a life especially near to God and in fervent response to His love.

Entry into the Third Order came only after the seeker had at great pains sought to make restitution for any wrongs he had consciously committed. The novitiate lasted for a year. The members of the order wore cheap clothing, undyed and without ornamentation. They ate only two meals a day, except when at heavy manual labor. They spent so little time and money on themselves, that they had a surplus to pour into the Lord's work and they gave lavishly of both to those who seemed to be in the greatest need: to the sick, to prisoners, to the poor, to the bringing in of a neighbor's harvest, to the burial of the dead, to the work of peacemaking.

They refused to bear arms, to take oaths, or to submit disputes to secular tribunals. They bound themselves to a program of simple prayers at several points in the day. They went to confess their sins more often than was customary, and once a month they had a special meeting in the local church, where common concerns were discussed, where a special address was given by a visiting Franciscan or by the local clergy, and where the group frankly gave each other mutual help on the matter of grave personal faults.

This Third Order spread like good news throughout Italy and to every part of the continent, and it was a significant spiritual, social, and even economic force in the thirteenth and fourteenth centuries. Third Order Franciscans in every walk of life were an important leaven in the life of their times, until they relaxed their original zeal and became stiffly organized as an auxiliary church fraternity.

## The Ashram Movement

A good deal of interest has been aroused in the West by Gandhi's ashrams at Sabarmati and at Sevagram. Here are communities where groups of men and women have quickened their lives at all points for a nonviolent approach to social problems. This interest in Gandhi's ashrams has attracted attention to the whole ashram movement.

"The ashram," writes E. Stanley Jones, "really in India springs from the ancient forest schools, where a guru, or teacher, would go aside with his chelas, or disciples, and in corporate spiritual quest would search for God through philosophical thought and spiritual exercises." But this school is not to be confused with a monastery and there is no standard type of ashram. They belong to a native Indian pattern that "began in the forest, but many ashrams were and are in the heart of cities. It is the national soul of India expressing itself in religion, the central characteristic of which would be simplicity of life and an intense spiritual quest."

Stanley Jones describes an experiment that he and his colleagues have made with a Christian ashram in India. Their free corporate life is an attempt to combine the Indian spirit, "an inner poise, a spiritual sensitiveness, a love of simplicity, an emphasis on the gentler virtues, a spirit of devotion, an ascetic tinge," with the development of men of Christ-force. It is a corporate spiritual life, a shared economic life, with an equal distribution of all the chores, including scavenging, and a life of fellowship extending to the renunciation of secret criticism and a vow of complete frankness with one another. This has meant the development of willingness to receive gladly the suggestions even of the weakest. A draft of a sharp public reply to an unjust attack was submitted by Stanley Jones to the group. They considered it prayerfully and returned it to him with three words written in the margin: "Not sufficiently redemptive."

One day a week in the ashram is given to silence. Each member of the ashram has his own work to do outside the community. Life in the ashram is a corporate discipline and a strengthening fellowship which contributes to the members' growth in Kristagraha—Christ-force.

## The Society of Friends

The life of the religious community is an answer to the "good news" itself which invites men to enter into such an inward fellowship. The early Christian community knew vividly what it was "to be all with one accord in one place," to experience the visitation of the Spirit together, to be branches of a common vine, members of a common body, to partake of common meals together, to look forward to dwelling together in a Father's house of many mansions. To respond to the good news meant to join God's family here and now in some little local Christian fellowship that touched every side of their lives.

This fellowship is both prepared for by the Spirit and is itself a condition of preparation for the deepest working of the Spirit. When the members of a fellowship know one another, care for one another, visit one another in their homes, consult one another, hold one another up in the silence and feel responsibility before God for one another, then when they meet together for worship they are truly open as a corporate group for the deepest working of the Spirit.

The importance of the Society of Friends to the development of communities lies in the fact that the Society is designed to be such a fellowship, a lay body of those in whom the indwelling Christ is at work effecting revolutionary changes. Its form of worship and its method of arriving at corporate decisions in matters of business are generally conceded to operate best within groups that are made up of fewer than a hundred persons. The lay character of its ministry enables these small units to survive without being forced to gather large numbers in order to collect enough financial resources for the support of a professional minister and his staff.

Few Friends' meetings today, however, can claim to offer this ideal type of fellowship. Some people would even be bold enough to suggest that this fellowship does not exist because so many within the Society of Friends are not really sure that they want the Christian revolution to take place within them and within their world. An Indian jailer stamped a copy of the New Testament which a prisoner had requested, *not dangerous*. The Society of Friends and the Christian Church as a whole in its present condition of softness would be stamped *not dangerous* by the rival national, racial, and class religions that have sprung up in our day. What many of us want could best be described as "The Christian Revolution, Ltd.," and the limitations we would place upon it resemble those the Irish town fathers placed upon the plans for a new jail. First it had to be built on the site of the old jail. Second, it had to be built out of the materials of the old jail. Third, the old jail had to be kept in use until the new jail was completed.

As for those who are awake to the swift moving revolutions that are sweeping the world today and who see the danger of the Christian revolution both within and without as no barrier—where will they find a religious community in which worship is the culminating act of this broader vital fellowship?

This question I can best answer in terms of the fellowship to which I belong, the Society of Friends. Those who move about among Friends' groups today report that out of the college and university centers, out of the work camps, out of foreign service projects, out of the ranks of professional people, and, though more tentatively, out of the ranks of those who work with their hands, "there is a people waiting to be gathered." Men and women are asking: "Within your ranks can we find an intimate fellowship of those who have set themselves to bring about the Christian Revolution, people who are 'incorrigible Christians'? Is there in your company a place for us to be renewed and transformed by this inward power that a few of your number have seemed to find, or are you simply another formal, respectable, nonintrusive religious group?"

The answer to this question cannot be an abstract or ideal

answer. It must be honestly given in the concrete terms of a local group which these friends might come into or which they might form if there were none in their community. In spite of service oganizations and educational experiments in centers like Pendle Hill, the Society of Friends must still live or die by the character and quality of its local meetings. They are its base. All else is built on them. Are the local meetings "intimate fellowships of those who are about the Christian Revolution"? How can the meetings begin where they are and move toward this end?

There are at least three simple concrete steps which local meetings may take that will greatly assist the cultivation of this fellowship. While they are steps that grow out of the life of the Society of Friends, they are steps that can be taken as well by other religious groups.

### The Ministry of Hospitality

The revival of Christian hospitality in which the members of the group partake of food with one another is essential. Visitors and new members are especially grateful for this open hand of friendship. The increasingly elaborate meals which many consider it necessary to set before guests have made this hospitality difficult for persons in moderate circumstances, but a return to simplicity would help in bringing about the revival of this precious sacrament.

### The Ministry of Visiting

Members of the group should visit one another in the spirit of that fellowship which they have felt in the meeting for worship. There is no more convincing way of showing affectionate concern than by visiting others in this spirit. In religious bodies where all visiting is done by professional workers the lay members lose a precious privilege that might be theirs, for the visitor nearly always receives more than he gives. There is nothing more rewarding than this visiting, nothing that shows more clearly where inner need is, where opportunity lies. It is no accident that in religious bodies which employ a pastor, the man who visits and knows his group can hold them together by this tie far more effectively than by the brilliance of his spoken word. To establish new groups or to revive dying ones the first essential is to visit, and the second essential is to visit, and the third essential is to continue visiting. These visits help to draw the meeting for worship into a basic fellowship that can yield to the Spirit. If the members of a group know of difficulties that one or another in their midst may be facing, they can literally draw on the bank of God's healing power for that member.

## The Ministry of Small Fellowship Groups

It is not easy to describe the place of little friendship groups within larger religious bodies, for they are scarcely organized groups at all, and the least hint of formally "promoting" them would almost destroy their genius. Out of this hospitality and this visiting, however, there may quite naturally grow up a desire on the part of several members to gather in one another's homes, perhaps for a meal and for a quiet evening of conversation about their deepest concerns. These little fellowship groups often begin with five or six persons and may never grow to be larger than eight or ten. They must not be a burden, but should come to pass only when members of a meeting feel a desire to have fellowship on common concerns further than is posisble in the meeting for worship.

Teresa of Avila wrote in her *Life* of her longing for such a group.

I should be very glad, that as in these days men meet together to conspire against the Divine Majesty, and to propagate their wickedness and heresies, so we five who at present love each other in Christ should also endeavor sometimes to meet together, for the purpose of undeceiving each other, for conferring on the means of reforming ourselves, and of giving God the greatest pleasure. For no one knows himself so well as they know who see us, provided they truly love us and are anxious for our advancement.

My wife and I have been members of several such fellowships. Their membership has changed, they have not all been connected with our own meeting, but they have been to us of inestimable value. A few friends have dined together perhaps once a month and have then spent the evening talking, at first a little hesitantly but later with increasing freedom, of those things which the life we are trying to live is feeding on, or being sharpened by, or being eaten away by. One or another has often taken to such a group decisions on matters of vocation and of plans for the future upon which they have objectively given their judgment. We have built natural and enduring and really inward fellowship out of these occasions that have also been gay, joyous times together.

For the past ten years a group made up largely of women who carry heavy domestic and social responsibilities have felt themselves drawn to meet together regularly in Philadelphia during the week for an unhurried period of silent meditation and mutual exchange on the life of devotion. In times like these when world events, for those who bear a testimony against war, threaten to isolate them still more from the community at large, this kind of small fellowship group may become no longer an elective but a necessity.

Several of these fellowship groups have included periodic times of withdrawal to some quiet place where they could spend one or two or three days largely in silence, where they could "balance the budget," recover their sense of direction, be inwardly refreshed by the "larger leisure" in God's presence that such an opportunity affords, and return to their ordinary lives with a sense of gratitude.

In these groups larger surfaces of our lives are opened to each other and to God than could be opened in any other way. The groups will vary in character and in their immediate concerns. Some have undertaken common work projects, such as the renovation of a meetinghouse shed, the clearing up of the grounds, or the construction of some needed improvement for the community. The eighteenth century French Protestant pastor, John Frederick Oberlin, used to work with his parishioners one Saturday in each month constructing roads in the parish and ending the day by sharing the Lord's supper together. Meetings for worship in Quaker work camps where members of the group have been at manual labor together seem to take on a fresh reality, for they bring to the worship a fellowship already partly built through common work. I know of a group of shut-ins who have banded into a "fellowship of those who care" and who practice intercessory prayer at noon each day. A fellowship group may form the nucleus for deputational work to help to quicken into life some expiring church or meeting, or it may be the agent of sustaining the civil liberties of some group in the community who cannot itself protest the wrongs done it. In Stavanger, Norway, such a group concerned itself for the life of the inmates of the city jail, taking flowers for each cell, holding weekly musical services, visiting the families of the prisoners. A fellowship group may work out the curriculum of an adequate religious education program and undertake to furnish teachers from its number, or it may set itself to study psychotherapy or to try out some experiments in Franciscan simplicity, or it may concern itself especially with the cultivation of the personal devotional lives of its members.

When two or three persons have come to an inward experience and commitment to a new life, or when some person is passing through a great and crushing sorrow, or when a man and wife are losing a faith that was once vivid and are growing indifferent for lack of intimate and regular touch with others who now believe as deeply as they once did, or when anyone for any reason needs a personal touch that goes beyond that of regular meetings for worship, would it not mean much to have little intimate and congenial fellowship cells into which these people could be readily invited?

This idea is not new. The appearance of these little inner lay fellowship groups within the church in many different centuries speaks for their essential function. The Third Order of Franciscans, the Beguines, the Friends of God, the Brethren of the Common Life, the Valiant Sixty in the early Society of Friends, the Wesleyan Class Meetings, the conventicle groups within the German Pietist Churches, the nineteenth century missionary fellowship groups, the Bibel Forscher groups in Germany, who, I am told, furnished in one year thirty-five martyrs to the cause of conscientious objection: all these reveal the capacity for this intimate and more intense side of Christian fellowship appearing within the churches as cells that nourish the Christian body and recall it to its true stature.

### The Group Gathers to Work

There is genuine work to be done as we seat ourselves in a meeting for worship. Whether we enter into the pool of silence or whether we remain idly on the shore as mere spectators depends very largely upon our performance or our shirking of this work.

There is the work of stilling the body in order to get it out of the way. There is the stilling of the surface distractions of the mind that keep it darting after this and after that, instead of opening itself to the Inward Guide. No one can expect to do this all at once. An English girl, who has since become a writer, described to me her first meeting for worship at Old Jordans Meeting: "Using the silence was a good deal like walking a tightrope. I would take a few steps and then fall off. Then I would get back on again for a way, and then fall off again. But while I was on, it was wonderful."

Such outward distractions as noises or words can readily be woven directly into a prayer. The noise of an insistent auto siren may call up in us the prayer: "Oh, that I might be warned by an even louder siren of the dangers that continually beset my torpid and careless soul," and then be ignored. Distractions of the mind are more troublesome, but most of them can best be treated by making no attempt to resist them, by acknowledging their presence and sinking to a depth that is beneath them. Half a mile under the ocean there is calm, no matter what the agitation may be on the surface.

Even more helpful in meeting these distractions is the work of guiding the mind into areas that are natural to the prayer of quiet.

There is confession. In the silence, under the gaze of God, there comes a wave of consciousness of the betrayals, the broken resolves, the harsh words, the sins of postponement, the self-centered coldness that has walled us from the loving God and from our fellows. In the confessional of silent prayer I may unlock the secret chamber of my hidden thoughts that trouble me in the night when I lie down to sleep, and in this secret confessional in the presence of God there may come a work and a victory whose intensity defies description. Donn Byrne's words in *Destiny Bay* might be repeated: "There were great battles fought in great fields, but there was never a harder one than that between myself and myself in that little room."

A man came to a pastor, time after time, and promised that he would never drink again. At last the pledge was taken in a final form, and yet once again in the late evening the man appeared and said he must be allowed to have a drink or he would die. The pastor quietly told him to go home and die, and went on with his work. The next morning the man came with a new confidence in his face and said, "I died last night." The facing of hidden fears in the silent confessional, the dying to fear, letting God have His way, is part of our work there.

In the silent confessional, we ought to work through to a knowledge of what we most deeply want. If prayer is the soul's deepest desire, then we must find out what the desire actually is. Upon deeper scrutiny, what we thought we longed for most of all may prove to be something very different. How often a sufferer may pray that God relieve him of sleeplessness, when what he really wants is to face and settle the ugly conflict over a guilty act that must be set right before he can be at peace again. The sleeplessness is to the mind what pain is to the body, a precious message of alarm that there is something wrong needing immediate attention. It would be almost tragic if it stopped before he had got at the root of it. A girl in one of the work camps said at the end of the summer that she had come bent on transforming that underprivileged community into a cell of the new social order she was alive to spread. Now that the summer was over, she continued, she wanted to confess to the group that she had discovered that neither she nor most of the campers she knew had enough self-discipline to begin to live in a new social order, let alone to share it with others. In the work of the silent confessional there take place just such discoveries as to what we most deeply long for and what we truly need.

There is another workroom in the house of prayer. It is the place of intercessory prayer, prayer for others. Someone has called it "unselfishness in prayer." There we may work for those in our religious fellowship with an intensity that knows no limits, for in intercessory prayer we can hold up the needs of others and the longings we have for them as in no other way. Isaac Penington's words on intercessory prayer speak to our condition today:

Are they in a snare? Are they overtaken by a fault? Yea, are they in a measure blinded and hardened so that they can neither see nor feel as to this particular? Retire, sit awhile, and travail for them. Feel how life will arise in any of you and how mercy will reach towards them and how living words from the tender sense may be reached forth to their hearts deeply by the hand of the Lord for their good.

Here too we may work with the grain of God by holding up the sufferings of the world, by holding up specific situations and letting God identify us with them and increase our responsibility for them. A much loved workman was being feted in Reading, Pennsylvania, during the depression by a group of his fellows on some anniversary. After the speeches that lauded him, they called on him to speak. He got up and said, "My friends, after all this I would be the happiest man in the world tonight if I could forget the ten million of our fellows who are unemployed." By the work of intercession we refuse exemption, we are cut off from forgetting, and we become God's conscripts for the work of the alleviation of suffering. By the work of intercession, too, we co-operate with God's healing forces even when we may be denied other access to the situation.

Finally, there is in the work of prayer much that is as gay, as joyous, and as prized as a silent walk with one we love. That is the time of silent fellowship with God when we confess nothing, desire nothing, intercede for nothing, but simply enjoy Him in thankfulness for so matchless a Lover, in thankfulness simply for God Himself. Thomas Story wrote of this part of our work upon the occasion of his first visit to a Friends' meeting, "Yet my concern was much rather to know whether they were a people gathered under a sense of the enjoyment of God," and he recorded that he was glad to stay.

*Let God Work*

All through this work of ours in guiding the deeper reaches of our consciousness in meditation and intercession and adoration, there is likely to come an increasing consciousness that God is at hand, and the longing that not only our work but God's work shall be wrought in each worshiper and in the worshiping group. It is good to work. It is still better that our work should lead up to letting God work. It is good to pray. It is still better to be prayed *in*. "Be silent that the Lord who gave thee language may speak, for as He fashioned a door and lock, He has also made the key."

Often the very strenuousness and the wilfulness of our own prayers may hide God's work from us. A Swedish woman writer wanted God to tell her what the next stage in her career was to be, and at length with a surge of abandonment that broke through all of her reserves she seemed to feel God saying, "How could you expect me to speak when you have kept me gagged for so long?"

When we let God work in worship we may be brought to see things in new perspectives. The late Dick Sheppard, an English apostle of peace, told how he felt an illness coming on and was terrified at the prospect, for he had every hour of his time for weeks ahead booked with important appointments. That night he dreamed that a messenger approached the Lord God and said, "Dick Sheppard is about to be ill." And the Lord wrung his hands in horror and said, "Oh, whatever shall I do? Dick Sheppard is about to be ill." The absurdity of the dream lingered with him, and he awoke in the morning smiling at himself and at his indispensability complex, and quite at peace within. When we let God work in worship, the fevered cries of "I have work to do, God cannot let me die" are revealed for what they are. John Woolman in his *Journal* speaks of having been "brought low" in the silence. That is letting God work. When we let God work, we are often led step by step to learn what surrender means. To a strenuous soul who is sweeping the ocean back with a broom it may mean to stand still and let the waves break over him, to discover that when he yields to life all is not lost.

Nowhere may this make itself more evident than in the use of time. There will be no lessening of urgency, rather a heightening of it, for "today is the only measure of time remaining." Yet there may come with surrender to God's working an abundant sense of leisure. There may be found, as Natalie Victor so eloquently expresses it,

Twenty-four hours in which to do the one thing needful, instead of ten or twelve in which to do a dozen. . . . There will be time to place ourselves at the disposal of anyone in real need: no time to waste at the street corner. There will be time to play with the children, no time to be devising schemes for our own amusement. There will be time to read widely, deeply, generously; no time to waste on trivialities. . . . There will be time to pray long and passionately for the coming of the Kingdom: no time to question its present security or its ultimate triumph.

We may let God work when we yield to the reknitting of the worshiping community itself as the members are drawn nearer to the center and to each other. The community that has no such common experience to gather it into an inward fellowship as children of a single loving Father, has not yet experienced the deepest fellowship of all.

It is here in worship, then, that all of the preparative experiences of the religious community culminate. The common meals, the visiting, the groups for study, for meditation, for counseling, for common projects: all these things have prepared the soil for this religious fellowship. Worship is no longer merely a respectable outward association. It is soil that has been ploughed and harrowed and disked by these common experiences. It has been made open for the planting of the seed.

# 7

# RETHINKING QUAKER PRINCIPLES

*There are deeps in us all far below our ideas. . . . To discover how to vitalize and to flood with power this fundamental stratum of our being is, after all, to uncover one of the master secrets of life.*

RUFUS M. JONES

Historian of mysticism in religion, philosopher, religious thinker, worker in the field of international problems, the late Rufus Jones was the most widely known Friend of the twentieth century. Early in life convinced of the value of what he termed "firsthand religion," he set out with great personal warmth and vitality to impress the reality of it upon Friends and non-Friends alike. He spoke in countless meetings and churches and assemblies; he taught philosophy for thirty years at Haverford, edited Friends magazines, helped found the American Friends Service Committee and served as its first chairman, wrote innumerable articles and more than one hundred books. He was the source of the five-volume standard history of Quakerism, the rediscoverer of the unbroken history of Christian mysticism, and the stimulus for many persons to a deepened and expanded view of Truth. *Rethinking Quaker Principles* appeared in 1940.

It is not often that something wholly new comes to our world. We can probably say that something absolutely new never happens. The newest new form always bears some marks of the old out of which it sprung. The new, like the new moon, is born in the arms of the old. We have a new word for the breaking in of the new out of the existent old.

We call it a mutation. A mutation is a unique and unpredictable variation in the process of life. It is the unexpected appearance of a new type in an old order. It is a leap and not a mere dull recurrence of the past. Something emerges that was not here before, something that is not just the sum of preceding events. The universe is on the march and the march springs surprises. The procession of life looks more like a steeplechase than like a predictable and repeatable habit track.

The birth of the Society of Friends is one of these mutations. It was not, of course, an absolutely new religious movement. It had a definite setting and a well-marked background in history, but nothing just exactly like it ever existed before in the world. I want to make you see, if I can, why it emerged when it did and what was the distinct type that broke in on the stream of the Reformation movement which was in full flood in England in the seventeenth century when Quakerism was born. It is obvious, or should be, to everybody that there would have been no Society of Friends if there had not been a Puritan movement, and yet it is just as certain that the Quakers were not, properly speaking, Puritans.

Thomas Cartwright (1535-1603) is the historical father of Puritanism and throughout the entire reign of Queen Elizabeth he prayed and preached and worked for a radical reform of the Anglican Church, which seemed to him to be the Roman Catholic Church slightly fixed over and "simonized," but on the whole the old original model. Cartwright and the other Puritan creative leaders had two major concerns. They were first of all fervid exponents of Calvin's theological system. They took over his conception of God as the absolute sovereign of the universe, whose inscrutable will determines irresistibly everything that happens in the visible and invisible worlds. The Puritans took over, too, Calvin's conception of man in his fallen state as wholly de-

praved and corrupt and involved by the "Fall" in utter
moral ruin, a being wholly devoid of merit. They took over
also the view that man's possible deliverance is due entirely
to the grace and mercy of God revealed and made effective
through Christ's propitiatory offering on the Cross, by which
those who are elect and who accept the proferred means are
saved—all others are eternally lost and doomed to Hell. The
Bible, which reveals God's plan, they believed, is His one
and only communication to the human race, and contains all
that man can ever know or needs to know of God's will and
purpose.

The other urgent Puritan concern was the reorganization
of the Church. They believed that the plan for it was plainly
set forth in "the word of God." This plan was for the early
Puritans the Presbyterian system in place of the Episcopal
system, inherited from the hated Roman Church. Unfortu-
nately both the Episcopal and Presbyterian systems confronted the reader of the infallible New Testament. Acts
and St. John's Epistles describe the apostolic churches as led
and guided by "elders," that is, presbyters, while St. Paul's
epistles speak of bishops and deacons as the guides of the
primitive churches. Here was a plain difficulty with the infallible Plan. And some of the Puritans, notably those that
founded New England, discovered that the New Testament
set forth a third plan, a Congregational plan.

The trouble with this infallible Bible was that there were
so many ways of interpreting it, none of which ways seemed
infallible to those who had a different way. In 1611 this
Book was put into marvelous English and everybody read
it with growing love and wonder. The more they read it the
more difficult it became to make readers agree upon any
one final and infallible interpretation of it. Honest minds
strangely differed about what it meant, and no one Plan
stood out as clearly revealed to everybody.

By 1643, when George Fox started out in his leather

breeches as a "seeker," there was a vast confusion of plans. Archbishop Laud had been executed and Episcopacy had suffered a great defeat. The Puritans were in control of Parliament. Presbyterianism was dominant and England was fighting a civil war. The longer they fought the more the confusion spread. There was almost from the first a strong popular reaction against Presbyterianism as a state church, and a vast variety of religious views and new church systems swarmed over England. In the midst of the confusion there broke out a powerful wave of mystical life and thought and religion, nowhere more in evidence than in the army of the Commonwealth, and especially in the mind of Cromwell himself. Little groups formed in many parts of England, opposed to infallible systems and intolerant authority, inspired by the writings of mystics on the continent, kindled by the freedom of the Gospel and resolved to create a new and freer type of spiritual religion for the future. That was a unique situation, and it only needed a creative leader to turn this unorganized and chaotic spiritual yearning into a high tide movement. George Fox was the prophet-leader who did just that in this hour of crisis.

Fox had almost certainly become unsettled in his religious views during his apprenticeship in Nottinghamshire, where he kept sheep, and when he came home and heard the extreme Calvinism of the "priest" of the Drayton Church, Nathaniel Stephens, he plainly revolted from what he called the "notions," and what we should call the "ideology," of the Calvinistic preaching which he was constantly hearing. At the age of nineteen he reached a stage of complete revolt, cut loose forever from the organized Church of his time, and went out on his feet as a desperate seeker for reality, for something that would "speak to his condition." Everywhere on his travels he found the preachers whom he met "hollow and empty." You must remember that the persons he calls "priests" were Presbyterian ministers. As he wandered about, however, he gathered up from "tender" people a great many fresh ideas and transforming insights. He saturated himself with the New Testament and the prophets, and little by little, during the four years of his wanderings, he began to have great mystical experiences of Christ's direct work on his soul, of God's enveloping love, and of the authentic reality of the pentecostal power of the Spirit. These experiences, which he called "openings," gave him an unparalleled degree of certainty and a convincing power. In fact, his religious experiences give him a place in the list of the foremost Christian mystics of history.

By 1647 he knew that he had found what he sought, and from that time on he began to gather kindred spirits around him—remarkable persons like Elizabeth Hooton, James Nayler, Richard Farnsworth and William Dewsbury. They were his first disciples. Five years later—in 1652—he found, in the neighborhood of Pendle Hill, "a great people to be gathered," and an immense convincement followed, which marks the birth of Quakerism as a successful movement. Out of the convincement of the northern "seekers" he secured Swarthmoor Hall as the center of his mission, and sixty highly qualified "Publishers of Truth" to assist him in proclaiming the Quaker message. The visit to Pendle Hill is the epoch-making event in Quaker history.

At this stage, organization of the movement was hardly thought of. The thrilling thing was the certainty of God's light and love in the individual's soul. The day dawn and the day star had risen in their hearts; that was enough. They knew that the light of Christ had broken in on their souls and they called themselves "Children of the Light." They no more felt the need of an organization than two young lovers do, or than the members of a happy family do. They

sat down in intimate worship together, tremulous with emo-
tion, and they let Christ take care of the result. There is no
doubt that they trembled and the name *Quaker* was given to
them, and stuck to them, because they actually *quaked*.
There was, too, a striking return to pentecostal experience
of new spiritual life and power. Early Quakerism was an
intense mass movement of the pentecostal type. These people
had discovered a new energy.

"I saw the Light of Christ," Fox says, "that it shines
through all." "The ocean of Life and Light and Love flows
over all oceans of darkness." "One person in the power of
God can shake the world for ten miles around." Yes, for ten
thousand miles. The movement was spontaneous and dynamic and grew by spiritual contagion, like the early Franciscan movement, and it remained for a long period very
much like the Third Order of St. Francis. It grew amazingly
in the eight years between 1652 and 1660 and the number
of members leaped to about forty thousand in England alone
in that period.

There are no marks of church structure in this early
movement. Those who composed it had revolted from the
heavy hand of organization and from the rigidity of what
they called theological "notions." What seemed to them the
most certain fact of their own experience was the surge of
the Spirit within and the revealing light of Christ operating
in the soul. This was not a speculative theory. It was a thrilling, palpitating experience. They did not at this stage think
of themselves as a new sect, a new denomination. George Fox
himself said we belong to "what was before all sects." They
thought in all sincerity that they were the "seed," "the first
fruits" of Christ's restored and renewed universal Church
of the Spirit. This movement which they were launching
was to be essential Christianity, the thing itself. Of that no

Quaker in George Fox's lifetime doubted. Strangely enough it was not by any means an impossible dream.

If the movement was to grow and spread and multiply as a "seed" should do, it must be kept in the vital process of life and unfolding development; not arrested and hardened into system and formality. There was for a long period no rigid list of members. "All the faithful men and women (i.e. all who attended meetings with regularity) *whose faith stands in the power of God* have a right of membership," according to a minute of London Yearly Meeting of 1676. The movement was managed and directed by persons possessing "gifts" rather than by chosen officers. There was no clear differentiation of officials before the year 1725, which marks the second stage of Quakerism.

It is an interesting fact that even the degree of organization implied by the name "Society of Friends" does not appear before the Restoration, i.e. 1660. In fact, the first existing reference to the term "Society of Friends" is 1667. Before this date the members are loosely called "Children of the Light," or "the Seed," or "Friends," and by the world "Quakers." The word "Society" was chosen to express the ideal of Quaker simplicity in organization. It meant then what we mean now by "Fellowship"—a vital spiritual group. It avoided the memory and the suggestion of danger which the word "Church" connoted to their minds. They wanted to be removed as far as possible from the danger of corporate compulsion in all matters which concerned the individual's relation with God, and in the deep-lying and sacred issues of faith and practice. They were feeling after a genuine basis of spiritual liberty, equality, and fraternity. They were endeavoring to provide free and ample scope for the life and growth of the soul of man both upward and outward.

At this early stage, and throughout the period of George Fox's life, nobody either outside or inside the Quaker movement thought of it in terms of an organized Protestant denomination. It had no ordained officials. It had no formulated and recognized creed. It had no sacramental ordinances. The existing churches of the period, Roman Catholic, Anglican, Presbyterian, Baptist and Congregational, all considered no body of Christians a church without those three essential aspects, ordination, creed, sacraments.

In one other respect Friends of the early period deviated from all existing Protestant churches. They did not regard the scriptures as the infallible "Word of God." They loved these scriptures with their whole heart. One of George Fox's hostile critics admitted that if the Bible were lost it could have been reproduced from the memory of George Fox. They were all saturated in it and quoted it most aptly and effectively. But the ultimate authority for them was always Christ, the living Word of God, interpreted for them in the New Testament, but still abiding, and revealing Himself in their own souls as Guide, Light, and Leader. That was essentially their new message.

How George Fox himself felt about a creed comes to light very clearly in what he said and did and wrote when the Congregationalists adopted their "Declaration of Faith and Order" at the Savoy Conference in 1658. Fox says, in his *Journal*:

Before this time the church-faith (so-called) was given forth, which was said to have been made at the Savoy in eleven days' time. I got a copy before it was published, and wrote an answer to it; and when the church-faith was sold in the streets, my answer was sold also. This angered some of the Parliament men so that one of them told me, "they must have me to Smithfield." [i.e. to be burnt]. I told him, "I was above their fires and feared them not." Reasoning with him, I wished him to consider "had all people been without a faith these sixteen hundred years that now the priests [i.e. Congregational ministers] must make them one?" Did not [and this is the Quaker point of view]—Did not the apostle say that Jesus was the author and finisher of their faith? And since Christ Jesus was the author of the apostles' faith, of the church's faith in primitive times, and of the martyr's faith, should not all people look unto Him to be the author and finisher of their faith, and not to the priests? Much work we had about the priest-made faith.

In no uncertain note he indicates here that "priest-made faiths" or "council-made faiths," or "convention-made faiths" are mental constructions, ideologies (his word is "notions"), which tend to be congealed substitutes for the soul's personal discovery of Christ, and for a vital correspondence with the divine mind and will and guiding leadership.

It is true—only too true—that many times in a history of nearly three hundred years Friends have attempted to produce these man-made faiths. Once in Barbados, in a moment of weakness, George Fox himself signed a creedal letter, and in other times of crisis sporadic attempts have been made to hold the line at some fixed point of doctrine. But these "declarations" have always been temporary expedients. They have always failed to express the central and abiding core of life and faith of the onward moving Quaker movement.

It is also true that the Society of Friends has occasionally gravitated in the direction of becoming itself a rigid and congealed sect. The pressure from above, that is from the leaders of the Society, to turn the Friends into a solidified "peculiar people," with a fixed garb and form of speech, hedged about and isolated from "the world" by carefully devised regulations and testimonies, is still remembered by some of us. This happened in the second period, not in the first. It came from outside influences, especially from the powerful contemporary wave of quietism, rather than from the genius and spirit of early Quakerism. What happened was that nearly every aspect of life, including the direction of love and affection in mar-

riage and the height of one's gravestone after death, was
regulated. The Discipline was a hard and fast system, which
expected conformity. The elders in those days actually
"eldered," and stood like adamant for a well-defined *status
quo*. A rhythmic and cadenced tone of voice was expected
if the preaching was to possess unction. The message must
show no sign or indication of previous preparation. "Thou
shouldst not have been thinking," was the comment of an
elder to me in the early days of my ministry, and he represented a long and weighty tradition of control. The hard-
ening of the arteries of the Society was much in evidence in
my youth, and one saw that a "society" could become, in
fact had become, as rigid and inelastic as a stiffly organized
church might be.

Well, that epoch has ended. Which ideal—an open or a
closed type of religion—is to be the ideal of the future? Open
religion means a type that is uncongealed, fresh, free, formative and in vital contact with the creative stream of divine
life. Open religion has faith in the spiritual capacity of the
soul and confidence that God and man are akin and essentially
belong together. Open religion, therefore, is expectant, for-
ward-looking. It prizes the past, but believing profoundly
that God is a living God, it sees more yet of love and truth
and goodness before us. Its ultimate assurances are not in
books or creeds or formulations or arguments, but in the
soul's experience of the reality and Christlikeness of God. It
dares to leave religion free to grow with the growing world
and growing mind, and to sail the uncharted seas with God.
The Society of Friends in its early formative period was a
striking illustration of open religion. The day dawn and the
day star had arisen in the hearts of these "Children of the
Light," and they moved forward.

Closed religion, on the other hand, stands for the finality
of the formulations of the past. The returns are assumed to

be all in. Truth has been fully revealed "by them of old time." The function of religion of this type is to interpret the sacred deposit from the past, the truth once and for all time delivered. There is, I suppose, no existent church or denomination all of whose members are now committed to that backward-looking program. There are Christians of the open type in even the most conservative groups.

It seems to me to be a major issue for the Society of Friends as for other religious bodies today whether on the whole the emphasis is to be for this type of open, expectant religion, or whether it is to seek for comfortable formulations that seem to ensure safety, and that will be hostages against new and dangerous enterprises in the realm of truth. Are we charged with hope and faith and vision or are we busy endeavoring to coin repetitive phrases and to become secure resting places for the mind?

Our very life is at stake on these issues. There are obviously many persons who want their sects to be safe and rigid. They have lost faith in the leadership of a living Christ in communion with the soul of man. The recovery of this faith in the living Christ as an eternal presence is essential to the existence of vital religious bodies. We need once more to be able to say with a Christian in the second century: "Christ is forever being reborn in the hearts of His followers."

I have insisted often enough that no significant movement can ever be understood until it is studied in the light of its historical background and its temporal setting. This is peculiarly true of the Quaker movement. George Fox was not the originator of a new stock of ideas and ideals. He was the convinced and dynamic interpreter—the articulate prophet, in fact, of a group of truths and principles that had long been in circulation. He became the effective organizer of a

Society, a beloved community, which incarnated and prop-
agated those truths and principles.

If I were to pick out one aspect of this Quaker way of life
which is most basic to it, I should choose the rugged feature
of sincerity. That trait characterized George Fox throughout
his entire life. There was a saying in circulation while Fox
was still an apprentice in Nottinghamshire—"If George says
*Verily,* there is no altering him." His father was known
throughout the region of Fenny Drayton as "righteous Chris-
topher," and the son exhibited throughout his life "the brave
old wisdom of sincerity." He found in his beloved Gospel
of John that doing the truth is the way into the light and he
inaugurated a Society that was first of all committed not to
saying but to doing the truth.

His hate of sham underlies a great many of his so-called
peculiarities. His refusal to take off his hat or to tip it as
a mark of honor to a human person was no doubt carried
to an extreme point of emphasis and proved to be the cause
of many severe prison sentences, but in all these things he
was uttering his powerful protest against the shams of hollow
fashionable manners. The same thing applies to his stark
simplicity of address and language. He would not pluralize
a single person. He would not use any form of compliment
unless he could use it with absolute honesty.[1]

Oliver Wendell Holmes has somewhere described minute
forms of life so transparent that one can look through their
bodies and see their hearts beat and their lungs breathe.
Such transparency of purpose, such purity of intention and

---

[1] These peculiarities of speech and of refusal to remove the hat, and the
further refusal to take any form of judicial oath, which cost an immense
amount of suffering, were not novelties introduced by George Fox. They
already were existing traits among "tender" people belonging to small mystical
groups in the Commonwealth era. At a later date these costly efforts to purify
manners of daily life and to scale them down to a basis of utter sincerity were
turned into the badges of a "peculiar people," and in the process they lost
their original meaning.

motive, was a feature of this effort of Fox to penetrate all etiquette and intercourse between persons with sincerity, and with the elimination of sham.

This sincerity and honesty, of course, applied to all business relations and dealings, but the principle went much deeper. It was a principle of life. You were to be through and through what you professed to be. There is a fine text in the Psalms: "Thou hast visited me in the night and searched me in the dark and thou hast found nothing wrong." I need hardly say that is a goal Quakers strive toward, not a terminus that has been reached.

It was on this same basis of sincerity that George Fox revolted from the use of theological "notions" and creedal statements, and brought religion down to a secure basis of experience, of life, of tested reality, and of discovered truth translated into action. To say or hear exalted phrases from a pulpit, or to sing hymns of lofty import, and then to go home and act precisely as though these exalted things had never been said, struck at his life, and threw him into a state of agony. It is impossible ever to estimate rightly the essential significance of the Quaker movement without a clear appraisal of the importance of this call to stark sincerity. And this call to sincerity lies at the root of the Quaker attempt to live the simple life. There is no fixed standard of simplicity. What is very simple for one person often seems very complex and extravagant for another person. There is no known calculus of simplicity. Simplicity at its best and truest is this utter honesty of heart and life, this complete sincerity of soul before God and in relation with our fellow men so that we truly struggle to be what we tell God we want to be and what we profess in our social relations to be. A Quaker must get out and keep out of the ruts of duplicity and sham. That is a basic Quaker way of life which gets back to its original spirit.

The next basic trait which I shall select is the emphasis on spiritual nurture. If one may judge by the writers of Quaker journals—and I have read almost every one of them —it becomes evident that these pillar Friends rated spiritual nurture very near the top of the scale of Quaker virtue. It is indubitably the trait that has secured Quaker survival. In most of the Disciplines, the Queries—those silent confessionals of life—have asked questions like these: Do parents and those having care of youth early instruct them in the principles of Truth? Do you bring up your children in the nurture of the Truth? Every home was to be a vital center, a hotbed as it were, for the formation, the culture, the growth of the essential principles of the spiritual life. There is no substitute for the home as a nursery of the spirit.

Propagation of Quaker ideals of life was implicit rather than explicit, like the mathematics of the honeybee and the spider. It was done by contagion, by unconscious imitation. The important features were not so much explained as exhibited in life and action. You learned to live by being in the currents of life. The element of hush and silence is, of course, of vast importance in all these matters of nurture. Birthright is no doubt a poor word, but there was a certain richness of provision which went with it at its best. "Things provided came without the sweet sense of providing." You simply drew upon an inheritance which became yours as naturally as the mother's milk nourishes the child.

The unbroken stream of visiting Friends who came into every Quaker home was a unique method of carrying on and of heightening this enrichment of life in the home. Sooner or later the most eminent persons in the Society, both at home and abroad, came with their benediction of sweetness and light, and in the religious "opportunity" with the family, which was an essential feature of the visit, a season of refreshment from on high often attended it and left a rich deposit in the soul.

The extraordinary interest in education, which has always characterized Friends in every period, is the flowering out of this deep concern for spiritual nurture. Wherever the meeting house went, the Quaker school, if in any way possible, sprang up beside it. These schools in their first intention were invariably nurseries of spiritual culture. They informed the mind, but above everything else they fed and nourished the inner life of the child, and carried forward the nurture which the home had begun. Schools and colleges form one of the major Quaker contributions to the world. But it is necessary to ask once more very seriously in the silent confessional of the Queries: Do you still in these modern times in your homes and schools and colleges bring up your children and those under your care in the nurture of Truth?

What comes first to mind when the Quaker way of life is mentioned is, almost certainly, the Quaker faith in the sacredness of human life and the refusal to use violent methods of force to change situations that are manifestly evil. The Quaker has unmistakably committed his trust for moral and social victories to the *armor of light* and the *sword of the spirit*—to methods that may be called gentle. He has been pretty consistently the bearer of a testimony for peace and in a good degree he has been a peacemaker. He has suffered much for his unyielding opposition to war. But his attitude toward peace and war is not an isolated attitude. It springs out of a deeper inward soil. It is an essential aspect of a larger whole of life.

Here especially we need to remind ourselves of the background movements which prepared the spiritual climate for the Quaker way of life. The Waldenses from the twelfth century on had stoutly refused to fight or to take human life.

They based their scruple on definite texts of Scripture. They took the Sermon on the Mount as a new law to be strictly obeyed. The Third Order of St. Francis inaugurated a truce of God, since in its original intention no member of it might bear arms. The fourteenth century mystics were distinctly on the side of the angels in their desire to be instruments of the Spirit in the reformation of the Church and in the remaking of the world in gentle ways.

Erasmus inaugurated a new era in the testimony for peace. He is one of the profoundest advocates of the peace method that has ever interpreted it. He maintained that love and patience, innocence and justice, self-restraint and willingness to suffer and endure are the infallible credentials of a Christian. His powerful influence as a scholar and as an interpreter of the New Testament gave these brave ideas of his a new standing in the world. The early Anabaptists and the Spiritual Reformers, both of whom were contemporaries of Luther, show in a marked way the influence of the great mystics before them and of Erasmus who had awakened and inspired them. They went back, as Erasmus had done, not so much to texts of Scripture as to the whole spirit of the New Testament and to what seemed to them to be the way of Christ. This stream of thought had quietly flowed into England in diverse currents and was an essential aspect of many of the mystical groups of the Commonwealth era, when George Fox and William Dewsbury and James Naylor and Isaac Penington were finding their way into a new manner of life.

However this new warm stream of life and thought may have reached George Fox across the bogs and swamps of the time, he gave it a peculiar color and a curve of direction from his own unique insight and character. William Penn was right when he said that George Fox was "an original and no man's copy." He was saturated with the New Testament.

He had found his way deeply into the heart of the Gospel, and the light of Christ had broken into his soul with fresh illumination. "I saw the light of Christ," he says, "shine through all." As one in the order of the prophets he made a novel contribution of his own to the way of life which the mystics and humanists and spiritual reformers before him had heralded.

In mapping out his path in the early creative days he felt his way along by inward vision. He did not explicitly think it out with his head. He certainly did not rest his case on texts which served as legal commands, though he knew the texts well enough. From somewhere he had caught and formed a deep-lying philosophy of life, which it is much more important to capture than it is to quote his pithy sayings at critical moments. It seems to me that the main secret is found in his discovery that God and man are never sundered, are never separate entities. There is always a tiny isthmus which links man's soul to the divine eternal mainland to which it belongs. The approach to God is not primarily up through nature and the natural order; it is rather through the soul of man which is essentially spirit and, therefore, may commune with Spirit.

To be "saved" for these early Quakers did not mean escaping the fires of Hell and gaining an entrance through the pearly gates into a peaceful Heaven. It meant an inward transformation of spirit and way of life. It was the birth of a new love, a new passion for holy living, a hate of sin both within and without. Salvation was an actual spiritual conquest and a new dynamic of life.

This Quaker philosophy of life was not a speculation and it was more than a faith. It was a vivid experience. The Light from beyond actually broke in on them and flowed over all their darkness. They knew God experimentally. They felt the healing drop into their souls from under God's wings.

And with it came the assurance that this inward event was possible for everyone possessed of a soul made in God's image. If this be so then it follows as a corollary that every man is highborn, with immense possibilities, and is infinitely precious. He may muckrake in the dirt, but there is a crown of righteousness hovering above his head, if he would only look up and see it!

This estimate of human life is an essential feature of Quakerism, when one goes back to its headwaters. It was implicit rather than articulate, but it colored the whole Quaker attitude toward life and formed the spring and motive of the costly peace testimony. In an Epistle of the year 1659, George Fox wrote: "All Friends everywhere, who are dead to all carnal Weapons and have beaten them to pieces, stand in that which takes away the occasion of Wars, in the Power which saves men's lives, and destroys none, nor would have others [destroy]." He quotes no texts. He gives no reasons. He simply says Friends cannot do the things which war involves.

Quakerism, then, let us say, is a bold experiment, not merely in pacifism in the midst of warring peoples, but an experiment with patience and endurance to exhibit a way of life which implements this high estimate of man's divine possibilities, and which even in the fell circumstances of war and hate goes on with a service of love and a mission of good will, the condition of peace. Mahatma Gandhi has described his life work as "My Experiments with Truth." I should like to have that term applied to Quaker service: "The Quaker Experiments with Truth."

Friends who have seen the significance of this experiment, this way of life, can be counted on to be purveyors of peace, both in peacetime and in wartime. They will not fight nor be entangled in the mechanisms of war. They will be calm and heroic in other ways. They will make heavy sacrifices to transmit their faith in services of love. They will die if it will demonstrate their faith and their truth. But they will not endorse war methods or voluntarily take part in a system that is engaged in carrying on war. There ought to be a world like this diviner one of which the Quakers dream; and they propose to go on living for it, suffering for it, and if necessary, dying for it. The testimony I am talking about is not negative. It does not begin with "Thou shalt not." It is first and last a positive and creative way of life and of enlarging the area of light and truth and love.

This spirit and way of life which explain the Quaker attitude to war lie also behind the humanitarian endeavors of Friends from the days of George Fox to the present time. That does not mean that Friends substitute love for force. They do believe that love is infinitely greater than force, but they know clearly enough that wrong social and economic conditions cannot be radically changed merely by loving those who are most responsible for the wrong, or by relieving the sufferings of those who are wronged. But the solution of the issues behind the ills of life can be better found, Friends believe, by those who work from the inside, who share sacrificially in the sufferings and who feel the burden of the tragic situations, than by those who stand off outside and merely apply a "magic" ideology.

Finally, here at the end, I shall put what might well have come first, the constant return of Friends to the springs and sources of life in worship. We may hold it as settled that we cannot change the world from ways of war to ways of peace, nor can we rebuild the social order on right lines for future generations, without the influence and guidance and inspiration of vital religion. A world built on purely secular lines would be a world that would fester and spoil and corrupt as has always happened. We must above everything else find our way back to the springs of life and refreshment for the hearts and souls of men. Religious faith when it takes us back to the true source of power removes from the mind the peril of bewildering unsettlement. It turns water to wine. It brings prodigals home. It sets men on their feet. It raises life out of death. It turns sunsets to sunrises. It makes the impossible become possible. The master secret of life is the attainment of the power of serenity in the midst of stress and action and adventure.

One of the most significant contributions which the Quakers have made has been their discovery of the value of silent communion and their practice of it as a source of strength and equipment. They begin all their meals in silence. They open all their meetings with a time of quiet, even their meetings for business, and they approach every practical task with a period of hush. It may, I think, be taken as a demonstrated fact that hush and silence minister to a consciousness of mutual and reciprocal communion with God. The soul in these deep moments of quiet seems to be both giving and receiving—to be breathing in a diviner life, and to be pouring out in response its own highest and noblest aspirations and expectations. Different exponents of religious faith differ widely in their emphasis on what is essential in belief and form and practice, but the representatives of all faiths, of all communions, of all systems, or of none, might find themselves moved, quickened, vitalized, refreshed, and girded for the duties and tasks of life by periods of expectant, palpitating hush with others who are fused together into one group of worshiping men and women.

Since the first world war, we have had many experiences of silence, in which a whole city, or even an entire nation, seemed somehow to find itself unified through an awe-inspiring hush, and more than that, to be lifted into communion with a vast invisible fellowship and with the Father of us all. It has well been called "the way of wonder," and I would add that it is the way of expectancy. Sometimes it

may be as important to get away from the problems of thinking as it is to get away from the yoke of business, or the press
of the crowd. There is as much need of a holiday from the
problems of the mind as there is for relief from hurry and
worry and grind of work.

There are deeps in us all far below our ideas. There is in
fact a substratum which is the mother-soil out of which all
our ideas and purposes are born, as capes of cloud are born
out of the viewless air. To feed or to fertilize that subsoil of
our conscious life is far more important than to capture
and to organize a few stray thoughts. To discover how to
vitalize and to flood with power this fundamental stratum of
our being is, after all, to uncover one of the master secrets
of life. Just that is what seems to happen to some of us in the
hush and mystery of intimate contact with divine currents,
in the living silence of corporate worship.

It is like a ship in a lock. Here the ship is, shut in by
great gates before and behind. Its driving engines have slowed
down; its speed has diminished to naught. It is no longer
going anywhere. And yet all the time the water is rising
underneath the ship, and when the gate in front swings open,
and the ship emerges from its period of full stop, it will go
out for its journey on a higher level and carry its burden of
freight henceforth on a new plane.

I have read of a nurse who, during the influenza epidemic
of 1918, became utterly worn out and incapable any longer
of coherent effort. One day when at the limit of herself, she
resolved to slip away and sit in quiet with a group of worshipers. She did so. The result was that the whole current
of her life was altered in the hour of genuine worship.
She felt herself restored, calmed and rebuilt. She returned to
her work with a freshness of spirit, a renewed will, and she
found herself raised to a new level of life and action, like
the ship emerging from the lock.

There are moments when the walls between the seen and

unseen appear to grow thin and almost vanish away, and one feels himself to be in contact with more than himself. The threshold of consciousness, which in our attentive and focussed states of mind bars the entrance of everything that does not fit the business in hand, drops to a different level and allows a vastly widened range of experience, and we suddenly discover that we can draw upon more of ourself than at other times. And in these best moments of widened range when we share the co-operative influence of many expectant worshipers around us, it seems often as though streams of life and light and love and truth flow in from beyond our margins, and we come back to work and business and thought again, not only calmed, rested, and made serene, but also more completely organized and vitalized and equipped with new energies of the spirit.

This hush and silence, therefore, of which I have been speaking, must be thought of as preparation and fortification for the main business of life. John Woolman, one of the humblest men that ever lived, became a veritable dynamo against the evil of slavery. He describes how he learned to wait in patience and to dwell deep in the life and love of God, and then when the time came for speech or action, he was prepared to "stand as a trumpet through which the Lord speaks."

The sensitiveness of the compass needle to the magnetic currents in which it moves reveals the fact that it has not only been carefully balanced on its pivot, but that it has also itself been magnetized and transformed through all its molecules. Somewhat so the dynamic worker at the tasks of the world must be organized within, must be brought into parallelism with celestial currents and be penetrated with energies beyond himself.

My beloved teacher, Josiah Royce, used to tell of an experience and a conviction which enables a man "to stand

anything that can happen to him in the universe." But we
must do more than stand the waterspouts which break over
us and rage around us. Our task is to bind up the broken-
hearted, to be a cup of strength in times of agony, to set
men on their feet when the foundations seem to be caving
in, and to feed and comfort the little children amidst the
wreckage of war and devastation. Those who are to do such
service need to know:

> That God at their fountains
> Far off hath been raining.

# 8

# CHRISTIANITY AND
# CIVILISATION

*If religion is a chariot, it looks as if the wheels on which it mounts towards Heaven may be the periodic downfalls of civilisations on Earth. It looks as if the movement of civilisation may be cyclic and recurrent, while the movement of religion may be on a single continuous upward line.*

ARNOLD J. TOYNBEE

One of the great intellectual projects of our time is Arnold J. Toynbee's *A Study of History*, a work of some thirteen parts in nine volumes which has been in progress since 1927. Two-thirds complete in 1939, it was interrupted by demands upon the author's knowledge during the war; publication of the concluding volumes is now awaited. Arnold Toynbee has lectured widely in England and in the United States; he is Director of Studies of the Royal Institute of International Affairs, Research Professor of International History at the University of London; his American headquarters are the Institute for Advanced Study. The lecture, *Christianity and Civilisation*, a great and profound statement of the Christian idea in terms of the flow of history, was first published in the United States by Pendle Hill in 1947. It is included in the excellent volume of Toynbee essays, *Civilisation on Trial*, published by the Oxford University Press, New York.

In A.D. 1950 the fortunes and future of the peoples of Western Europe are still a matter of concern to the world as a whole, because this little patch of territory on the extreme edge of the vast Eurasian Continent has been the seed-bed of the Western Civilisation that now overshadows the Earth.

The decline of Western Europe—if she really were to fall into a lasting decay—might still be as serious for the prospects of civilisation as was the decline of Greece in the last centuries B.C. Yet the experience of even that brief span of five or six thousand years within which we have seen civilisations rising and falling so far, is sufficient to show us that these ups and downs in the level of secular social life are not the true barometer of Man's success and failure. Our secular life in this world is only a fragment of some larger life of higher spiritual dimensions, and there is no reason for supposing that the spiritual welfare of the kingdom of God is jeopardised by our temporal misfortunes in this world. Indeed, in so far as human understanding in this life can grasp the relation between these two intersecting worlds, in both of which we have a footing, it looks as if our tribulations on the secular plane were actually opportunities for achievement in the spiritual sphere.

This is the subject which the present essay tries to broach. In these few pages it is only possible to raise one or two of the questions that arise, and indeed one might write volumes without arriving at the answers. Complete and perfect answers are, we must frankly confess, most unlikely ever to be attainable under the conditions of this life, for, just because we are grappling here with the most important issue in human life, we are at grips with something that transcends the limits of human understanding and experience. Since Man first found himself passing, as a pilgrim and a sojourner, through this world, he has always had to live by faith; for, without perpetually taking action, he cannot live at all, and he cannot wait to act until he has attained that fullness of knowledge which is always beyond his reach.

From time to time Man has made additions to his knowledge that have been extensive by comparison with the size of the area already reclaimed. A case which looms large to

us today is the recent advance in our understanding of—
and consequent control over—the workings of physical nature. Yet such advances in our knowledge no more appre-
ciably diminish the infinite expanse of our ignorance than
the expanse of the Atlantic Ocean has been diminished
by the Bostonians' feat of filling in their Back Bay; and our
ocean of ignorance is deep as well as broad; for we have
been more successful in exploring the fringes of the physical
surface of the universe than in plumbing its spiritual depths.
Our modern Western advance in the understanding of physical nature has not been accompanied by any corresponding
increase in spiritual enlightenment. In our knowledge of ourselves and our knowledge of God—the two fields of knowledge that are all-important for us—the founders of the
higher religions are still the pioneers; and none of these
benefactors of Mankind are either Western or modern. The
universe as we see it through contemporary Western eyes is
not the true picture of the universe as it is. In the perspec-
tive even of a distant future in this world, it will probably
come to seem fantastically out of focus. From the eternal
standpoint of God, we may be sure that it is no more than a
mirage. This illusion is the greatest obstacle to our salvation even on the secular plane of life; but we do know at any
rate the direction in which we have to move in our search
for a less misleading angle of vision. We have to shift our
attention from physical nature to the life of the spirit; from
the creature to the Creator.

The relation between Christianity and civilisation is a
question which has always been at issue since the foundation of the Christian Church, and of course there have been
a number of alternative views on it. One of the oldest and
most persistent views is that Christianity was the destroyer
of the civilisation within whose framework it grew up. That

was, I suppose, the view of the Emperor Marcus, as far as he was aware of the presence of Christianity in his world. It was most emphatically and violently the view of his successor, the Emperor Julian, and it was also the view of the English historian Gibbon, who recorded the decline and fall of the Roman Empire long after the event. In the last chapter of Gibbon's history there is one sentence in which he sums up the theme of the whole work. Looking back, he says: "I have described the triumph of barbarism and religion," meaning that Christianity as well as the barbarian invaders played a part in the overthrow of the civilisation for which the Roman Empire stood.

One hesitates to question Gibbon's authority, but I believe there is a fallacy in this view which vitiates the whole of it. Gibbon assumes that the Graeco-Roman civilisation stood at its height in the second century and that in tracing its decline from that moment he is tracing that decline from the beginning. Evidently, if you take that view, Christianity rises as the empire sinks, and the rise of Christianity is the fall of civilisation. I think Gibbon's initial error lies in supposing that the ancient civilisation of the Graeco-Roman world began to decline in the second century after Christ. I think it really began to decline in the fifth century before Christ. It died, not by murder, but by suicide; and that act of suicide was committed before the fifth century B.C. was out. It was not even the philosophies which preceded Christianity that were responsible for the death of the ancient Graeco-Roman civilisation. The philosophies arose because the civic life of that civilisation had already destroyed itself by turning itself into an idol to which men paid an exorbitant worship. And the rise of the philosophies, and the subsequent rise of the religions out of which Christianity emerged as the final successor of them all, was something that happened after the Graeco-Roman civilisation had already put itself to death. The rise of the philosophies and that of the religions was not a cause; it was a consequence.

When Gibbon in that opening passage of his work looks at the Roman Empire in the second century, he does not say explicitly—but I am sure this was in his mind—that he is also thinking of himself as standing on another peak of civilisation and looking back towards that distant peak in the past across a broad trough of barbarism in between. Gibbon thought to himself:

On the morrow of the death of the Emperor Marcus the Roman Empire went into decline. All the values that I, Gibbon, and my kind care for began then to be degraded. Religion and barbarism began to triumph. This lamentable state of affairs continued to prevail for hundreds and hundreds of years; and then, a few generations before my time, no longer ago than the close of the seventeenth century, a rational civilisation began to emerge again.

From his peak in the eighteenth century Gibbon looks back to the peak in the second century, and that view—which is, I think, implicit in Gibbon's work—has been put very clearly and sharply by a writer of the twentieth century, from whom I propose to quote a passage somewhat at length because it is, so to speak, the formal antithesis of the thesis which I want to maintain.

Greek and Roman society was built on the conception of the subordination of the individual to the community, of the citizen to the state; it set the safety of the commonwealth, as the supreme aim of conduct, above the safety of the individual whether in this world or in a world to come. Trained from infancy in this unselfish ideal, the citizens devoted their lives to the public service and were ready to lay them down for the common good; or if they shrank from the supreme sacrifice, it never occurred to them that they acted otherwise than basely in preferring their personal existence to the interests of their country. All this was changed by the spread of Oriental religions which inculcated the communion of the soul with God and its eternal salvation as the only objects worth living for, objects in comparison with which the prosperity and even the existence of the state sank into insignificance. The inevitable result of this selfish and immoral doctrine was to withdraw the devotee more and more from the public service, to concentrate his thoughts on his own spiritual emotions, and to breed in him a contempt for the present life which he regarded merely as a probation for a better and an eternal. The saint and the recluse, disdainful of earth and rapt in ecstatic contemplation of heaven, became in popular opinion the highest ideal of humanity, displacing the old ideal of the patriot and hero who, forgetful of self, lives and is ready to die for the good of his country. The earthly city seemed poor and contemptible to men whose eyes beheld the City of God coming in the clouds of heaven. Thus the center of gravity, so to say, was shifted from the present to a future life, and however much the other world may have gained, there can be little doubt that this one lost heavily by the change. A general disintegration of the body politic set in. The ties of the state and the family were loosened: the structure of society tended to resolve itself into its individual elements and thereby to relapse into barbarism; for civilisation is only possible through the active cooperation of the citizens and their willingness to subordinate their private interests to the common good. Men refused to defend their country and even to continue their kind. In their anxiety to save their own souls and the souls of others, they were content to leave the material world, which they identified with the principle of evil, to perish around them. This obsession lasted for a thousand years. The revival of Roman law, of the Aristotelian philosophy, of ancient art and literature at the close of the Middle Ages, marked the return of Europe to native ideals of life and conduct, to saner, manlier views of the world. The long halt in the march of civilisation was over. The tide of Oriental invasion had turned at last. It is ebbing still.

It is ebbing indeed! And one might speculate about what the author of this passage, which was first published in 1906, would now write if he were revising his work for a fourth edition today. I have not yet mentioned the author's name; but, for those who do not know it already, I would say that it is not Alfred Rosenberg; it is Sir James Frazer. I wonder what that gentle scholar thinks of the latest form in which Europe's return "to native ideals of life and conduct" has manifested itself.

Now you will have seen that the most interesting thesis in that passage of Frazer's is the contention that trying to save one's soul is something contrary to, and incompatible with, trying to do one's duty to one's neighbour. I am going to challenge that thesis; at the moment I merely want to point out that Frazer is at the same time putting Gibbon's thesis and stating it in explicit terms; and on this point I would give Frazer the answer that I have already ventured to give to Gibbon: that Christianity was not the destroyer of the ancient Greek civilisation, because that civilisation had decayed from inherent defects of its own before Christianity arose. But I would agree with Frazer, and would ask you to agree with me, that the tide of Christianity has been ebbing and that our post-Christian Western secular civilisation that has emerged is a civilisation of the same order as the pre-Christian Graeco-Roman civilisation. This observation opens up a second possible view of the relation between Christianity and civilisation—not the same view as that held in common by Gibbon and Frazer, not the view that Christianity has been the destroyer of civilisation, but an alternative view in which Christianity appears in the role of the humble servant of civilisation.

According to this second possible view, Chrisianity is, as it were, the egg, grub and chrysalis between butterfly and butterfly. Christianity is a transitional thing which bridges the gap between one civilisation and another, and I confess that I myself held this rather patronising view for many years. On this view you look at the historical function of the Christian Church in terms of the process of the reproduction of civilisations. Civilisation is a species of being which seeks to reproduce itself, and Christianity has had a useful but a subordinate role in bringing two new secular civilisations to birth after the death of their predecessor. You find the ancient Graeco-Roman civilisation in decline from the close of the second century after Christ onwards. And then after an interval you find a new secular civilisation arising out of the ruins of its Graeco-Roman predecessor. And you look at the role of Christianity in the interval and conclude that Christianity is a kind of chrysalis which has held and preserved the hidden germs of life until these have been able to break out again into a new growth of secular civilisation. That is an alternative view to the theory of Christianity being the destroyer of the ancient Graeco-Roman civilisation; and, if one looks abroad through the history of civilisations, one can see other cases which seem to conform to the same pattern.

Now I think there is perhaps a chysalis-like element in the constitution of the Christian Church—an institutional element that I am going to deal with later—which may have quite a different purpose from that of assisting in the reproduction of civilisations. But before we accept at all an account of the place and role of Christianity and of the other living religions in social history which represents these religions as being mere instruments for assisting in the process of the reproduction of civilisations, let us go on testing the hypothesis by examining whether, in every instance of the parent-and-child relation between civilisations, we find a chrysalis-church intervening between the parent civilisation and the daughter civilisation.

On this test, we shall seem to find no higher religion at all between primitive societies and civilisations of the first generation, and between civilisations of the first and those of the second generation either none or only rudiments. It is between civilisations of the second and those of the third generation that the intervention of a higher religion seems to be the rule, and here only.

If there is anything in this analysis of the relation between civilisations and higher religions, this suggests a third possible view of that relation which would be the exact inverse of the second view which I have just put before you. On that second view, religion is subsidiary to the reproduction of secular civilisations, and the inverse of that would be that the successive rises and falls of civilisations may be subsidiary to the growth of religion.

The breakdowns and disintegrations of civilisations might be stepping-stones to higher things on the religious plane. After all, one of the deepest spiritual laws that we know is the law that is proclaimed by Aeschylus in the words "it is through suffering that learning comes," and in the New Testament in the verse "whom the Lord loveth, He chasteneth; and scourgeth every son whom He receiveth." If you apply that to the rise of the higher religions which has culminated in the flowering of Christianity, you might say that the Passion of Christ was the culminating and crowning experience of the sufferings of human souls in successive failures in the enterprise of secular civilisation. The Christian Church itself arose out of the spiritual travail which was a consequence of the breakdown of the Graeco-Roman civilisation. Again, the Christian Church has Jewish and Zoroastrian roots, and those roots sprang from an earlier breakdown, the breakdown of a Syrian civilisation which was a sister to the Graeco-Roman. The kingdoms of Israel and Judah were two of the many states of this ancient Syrian world; and it was the premature and permanent overthrow of these worldly commonwealths, and the extinction of all the political hopes which had been bound up with their existence as independent polities, that brought the religion of Judaism to birth and evoked the highest expression of its spirit in the elegy of the Suffering Servant which is appended in the Bible to the book of the prophet Isaiah. Judaism, likewise, has a Mosaic root which in its turn sprang from the withering of the second crop of the ancient Egyptian civilisation. I do not know whether Moses and Abraham are historical characters, but I think it can be taken as certain that they represent historical stages of religious experience, and Moses' forefather and forerunner Abraham received his enlightenment and his promise at the dissolution, in the seventeenth or early sixteenth century before Christ, of the ancient civilisation of Sumer and Akkad—the earliest case, known to us, of a civilisation going to ruin. These men of sorrows were precursors of Christ; and the sufferings through which they won their enlightenment were Stations of the Cross in anticipation of the Crucifixion. That is, no doubt, a very old idea, but it is also an ever new one.

If religion is a chariot, it looks as if the wheels on which it mounts towards Heaven may be the periodic downfalls of civilisations on Earth. It looks as if the movement of civilisation may be cyclic and recurrent, while the movement of religion may be on a single continuous upward line. The continuous upward movement of religion may be served and promoted by the cyclic movement of civilisations round the cycle of birth–death–birth.

If we accept this conclusion, it opens up what may seem a rather startling view of history. If civilisations are the handmaids of religion and if the Graeco-Roman civilisation served as a good handmaid to Christianity by bringing it to birth before that civilisation finally went to pieces, then the civilisations of the third generation may be vain repetitions of the Gentiles. If it is the historical function of civilisations to serve, by their downfalls, as stepping stones to a

progressive process of the revelation of always deeper religious insight, and the gift of ever more grace to act on this
insight, then the societies of the species called civilisations
will have fulfilled their function when once they have
brought a mature higher religion to birth; and, on this
showing, our own Western post-Christian secular civilisation
might at best be a superfluous repetition of the pre-Christian Graeco-Roman one, and at worst a pernicious back-
sliding from the path of spiritual progress. In our Western
world of today, the worship of Leviathan—the self-worship
of the tribe—is a religion to which all of us pay some
measure of allegiance; and this tribal religion is, of course,
sheer idolatry. Communism, which is another of our latter-
day religions, is, I think, a leaf taken from the book of Christianity—a leaf torn out and misread. Democracy is another
leaf from the book of Christianity, which has also, I fear,
been torn out and, while perhaps not misread, has certainly
been half emptied of meaning by being divorced from its
Christian context and secularised; and we have obviously,
for a number of generations past, been living on spiritual
capital: I mean clinging to Christian practice without possessing the Christian belief. Practice unsupported by belief
is a wasting asset, as we have suddenly discovered, to our
dismay, in this generation.

If this self-criticism is just, then we must revise the whole
of our present conception of modern history; and if we can
make the effort of will and imagination to think this in-
grained and familiar conception away, we shall arrive at a very
different picture. Our present view of modern history focuses
attention on the rise of our modern Western secular civilisation as the latest great new event in the world. As we follow
that rise through the Renaissance to the eruption of democracy and science and modern scientific technique, we think
of all this as being the great new event in the world which

demands our attention and commands our admiration. If we can bring ourselves to think of it, instead, as one of the vain repetitions of the Gentiles—an almost meaningless repetition of something that the Greeks and Romans did before us and did supremely well—then the greatest new event in the history of mankind will be seen to be a very different one. The greatest new event will then not be the monotonous rise of yet another secular civilisation out of the bosom of the Christian Church in the course of these latter centuries; it will still be the Crucifixion and its spiritual consequences. There is one curious result of our immense modern scientific discoveries which is, I think, often overlooked. On the vastly changed time-scale which our astronomers and geologists have opened up to us, the beginning of the Christian era is an extremely recent date; on a time-scale in which nineteen hundred years are no more than the twinkling of an eye, the beginning of the Christian era is only yesterday. It is only on the old-fashioned time-scale, on which the creation of the world and the beginning of life on the planet were reckoned to have taken place not more than six thousand years ago, that a span of nineteen hundred years seems a long period of time and the beginning of the Christian era therefore seems a far-off event. In fact it is a very recent event—perhaps the most recent significant event in history—and that brings us to a consideration of the prospects of Christianity in the future history of mankind on Earth.

On this view of the history of religion and of the civilisations, it has not been the historical function of the Christian Church just to serve as a chrysalis between the Graeco-Roman civilisation and its daughter civilisations in Byzantium and the West; and supposing that these two civilisations, which are descended from the ancient Graeco-Roman one, turn out to be no more than vain repetitions of their parent, then there will be no reason to suppose that Christianity itself will be superseded by some distinct, separate and different higher religion which will serve as a chrysalis between the death of the present Western civilisation and the birth of its children. On the theory that religion is subservient to civilisation, you would expect some new higher religion to come into existence on each occasion in order to serve the purpose of tiding over the gap between one civilisation and another. If the truth is the other way round—if it is civilisation that is the means and religion that is the end—then, once again, a civilisation may break down and break away, but the replacement of one higher religion by another will not be a necessary consequence. So far from that, if our secular Western civilisation perishes, Christianity may be expected not only to endure but to grow in wisdom and stature as the result of a fresh experience of secular catastrophe.

There is one unprecedented feature of our own post-Christian secular civilisation. In the course of its expansion our modern Western secular civilisation has become literally world-wide, and has drawn into its net all other surviving civilisations as well as primitive societies. At its first appearance Christianity was provided by the Graeco-Roman civilisation with a universal state, in the shape of the Roman Empire with its policed roads and shipping routes, as an aid to the spread of Christianity round the shores of the Mediterranean. Our modern Western secular civilisation in its turn may serve its historical purpose by providing Christianity with a completely world-wide repetition of the Roman Empire to spread over. We have not quite arrived at our Roman Empire yet. But, long before a world is unified politically, it is unified economically and in other material ways; and the unification of our present world has long since opened the way for St. Paul, who once travelled from the Orontes to the Tiber under the aegis of the Pax Romana, to travel on from the Tiber to the Mississippi and from the

Mississippi to the Yangtse, while Clement's and Origen's work of infusing Greek philosophy into Christianity at Alexandria might be emulated in some city of the Far East by the infusion of Chinese philosophy into Christianity. This intellectual feat has indeed been partly performed already. One of the greatest of modern missionaries and modern scholars, Matteo Ricci, who was both a Jesuit father and a Chinese literatus, set his hand to that task before the end of the sixteenth century of the Christian era. It is even possible that as, under the Roman Empire, Christianity drew out of, and inherited from, the other Oriental religions the heart of what was best in them, so the present religions of India and the form of Buddhism that is practiced today in the Far East may contribute new elements to be grafted on to Christianity in days to come. And then one may look forward to what may happen when Caesar's Empire decays—for Caesar's Empire always does decay after a run of a few hundred years. What may happen is that Christianity may be left as the spiritual heir of all the other higher religions, from the post-Sumerian rudiment down to those that in A.D. 1950 are still living separate lives side by side with Christianity, and of all the philosophies from Ikhnaton's to Hegel's, while the Christian Church as an institution may be left as the social heir of all the other churches and all the civilisations.

That side of the picture brings one to another question which is both always old and always new—the question of the relation of the Christian Church to the Kingdom of Heaven. We seem to see a series of different kinds of society succeeding one another in This World. As the primitive species of societies has given place to a second species, known as the civilisations, within the brief period of the last six thousand years, so this second species of local and ephemeral societies may perhaps give place in its turn to a third species embodied in a single world-wide and enduring representative in the shape of the Christian Church. If we can look forward to that, we shall have to ask ourselves this question: Supposing that this were to happen, would it mean that the Kingdom of Heaven would then have been established on Earth?

I think this question is a very pertinent one in our day, because some kind of earthly paradise is the goal of most of the current secular ideologies. To my mind the answer is emphatically "No," for several reasons which I shall now do my best to put before you.

One very obvious and well-known reason lies in the nature of society and in the nature of man. Society is, after all, only the common ground between the fields of action of a number of personalities, and human personality, at any rate as we know it in This World, has an innate capacity for evil as well as for good. If these two statements are true, as I believe them to be, then in any society on Earth, unless and until human nature itself undergoes a moral mutation which would make an essential change in its character, the possibility of evil, as well as of good, will be born into the world afresh with every child, and will never be wholly ruled out as long as that child remains alive. This is as much as to say that the replacement of a multiplicity of civilisations by a universal church would not have purged human nature of original sin; and this leads to another consideration: so long as original sin remains an element in human nature, Caesar will always have work to do, and there will still be Caesar's things to be rendered to Caesar, as well as God's to God, in This World. Human society on Earth will not be able wholly to dispense with institutions of which the sanction is not purely the individual's active will to make them work, but is partly habit and partly even force. These imperfect institutions will have to be administered by a secular Power which might be subordinated to religious authority but would not thereby be eliminated. And even if Caesar were not merely subordinated but were wholly eliminated by the Church, something of him would still survive in the constitution of his supplanter; for the institutional element has historically, to date, been dominant in the life of the Church herself in her traditional Catholic form, which, on the long historical view, is the form in which one has to look at her.

In this Catholic form of the Church, I see two fundamental institutions, the Sacrifice of the Mass and the Hierarchy, which are indissolubly welded together by the fact that the priest, by definition, is the person with the power to perform the rite. If, in speaking of the Mass, one may speak, without offence, with the tongues of the historian and the anthropologist, then, using this language, one may describe the Sacrifice of the Mass as the mature form of a most ancient religious rite of which the rudiments can be traced back to the worship of the fertility of the Earth and her fruits by the earliest tillers of the soil. (I am speaking here merely of the mundane origin of the rite.) As for the Hierarchy of the Church in its traditional form, this, as one knows, is modelled on a more recent and less awe-inspiring yet nevertheless most potent institution, the imperial civil service of the Roman Empire. The Church in its traditional form thus stands forth armed with the spear of the Mass, the shield of the Hierarchy and the helmet of the Papacy; and perhaps the subconscious purpose—or the divine intention, if you prefer that language—of this heavy panoply of institutions in which the Church has clad herself is the very practical one of outlasting the toughest of the secular institutions of This World, including all the civilisations. If we survey all the institutions of which we have knowledge in the present and in the past, I think that the institutions created, or adopted and adapted, by Christianity are the toughest and the most enduring of any that we know and are therefore the most likely to last—and outlast all the rest. The history of Protestantism would seem to indicate that the Protestant act of casting off this armour four hundred years ago was premature; but that would not necessarily mean that this step would always be a mistake; and, however that may be, the institutional element in the traditional Catholic form of the Church Militant on Earth, even if it proves to be an invaluable and indispensable means of survival, is all the same a mundane feature which makes the Church Militant's life different from that of the Kingdom of Heaven, in which they neither marry nor are given in marriage but are as the angels of God, and in which each individual soul catches the spirit of God from direct communion with Him—"like light caught from a leaping flame," as Plato puts it in his Seventh Letter. Thus, even if the Church had won a fully world-wide allegiance and had entered into the inheritance of the last of the civilisations and of all the other higher religions, the Church on Earth would not be a perfect embodiment here on Earth of the Kingdom of Heaven. The Church on Earth would still have sin and sorrow to contend with as well as to profit by as a means of grace on the principle of "It is through suffering that learning comes," and she would still have to wear for a long time to come a panoply of institutions to give her the massive social solidity that she needs in the mundane struggle for survival, but this at the inevitable price of spiritually weighing her down.

The position in which the Church would then find herself is well conveyed in Plato's conceit, in the *Phaedo,* of the true surface of the Earth. We live, Plato suggests, in a large but local hollow, and what we take to be the air is really a sediment of fog. If one day we could make our way to the upper levels of the surface of the Earth, we should there breathe the pure ether and should see the light of the sun and stars direct; and then we should realise how dim and blurred had been our vision down in the hollow, where we see the heavenly bodies, through the murky atmosphere in which we breathe, as imperfectly as the fishes see them through the water in which they swim. This Platonic conceit is a good simile for the life of the Church Militant on Earth; but the truth cannot be put better than it has been by Saint Augustine.

It is written of Cain that he founded a commonwealth; but Abel—true to the type of the pilgrim and sojourner that he was —did not do the like. For the Commonwealth of Saints is not of This World, though it does give birth to citizens here in whose persons it performs its pilgrimage until the time of its Kingdom shall come—the time when it will gather them all together.

This brings me to the last of the topics on which I am going to touch, that of the relation between Christianity and progress.

If it is true, as I think it is, that the Church on Earth will never be a perfect embodiment of the Kingdom of Heaven, in what sense can we say the words of the Lord's Prayer: "Thy Kingdom come, Thy will be done on Earth as it is in Heaven"? Have we been right, after all, in coming to the conclusion that—in contrast to the cyclic movement of the rises and falls of civilisations—the history of religion on Earth is a movement in a single continuous upward line? What are the matters in which there has been, in historical times, a continous religious advance? And have we any reason to think that this advance will continue without end? Even if the species of societies called civilisations does give way to an historically younger and perhaps spiritually higher species embodied in a single world-wide and enduring representative in the shape of the Christian Church, may there not come a time when the tug of war between Christianity and original sin will settle down to a static balance of spiritual forces?

Let me put forward one or two considerations in reply to these questions.

In the first place, religious progress means spiritual prog-

ress, and spirit means personality. Therefore religious progress must take place in the spiritual lives of personalities—
it must show itself in their rising to a spiritually higher
state and achieving a spiritually finer activity.

Now, in assuming that this individual progress is what
spiritual progress means, are we after all admitting Frazer's
thesis that the higher religions are essentially and incurably
anti-social? Does a shift of human interest and energy from
trying to create the values aimed at in the civilizations to
trying to create the values aimed at in the higher religions
mean that the values for which the civilisations stand are
bound to suffer? Are spiritual and social values antithetical
and inimical to each other? Is it true that the fabric of
civilisation is undermined if the salvation of the individual
soul is taken as being the supreme aim of life?

Frazer answers these questions in the affirmative. If his
answer were right it would mean that human life was a
tragedy without a catharsis. But I personally believe that
Frazer's answer is not right, because I think it is based on a
fundamental misconception of what the nature of souls or
personalities is. Personalities are inconceivable except as
agents of spiritual activity; and the only conceivable scope for
spiritual activity lies in relations between spirit and spirit.
It is because spirit implies spiritual relations that Christian
theology has completed the Jewish doctrine of the Unity of
God with the Christian doctrine of the Trinity. The doctrine
of the Trinity is the theological way of expressing the revelation that God is a spirit; the doctrine of the Redemption is
the theological way of expressing the revelation that God
is Love. If Man has been created in the likeness of God,
and if the true end of Man is to make this likeness ever
more and more like, then Aristotle's saying that "Man is
a social animal" applies to Man's highest potentiality and
aim—that of trying to get into ever closer communion with

God. Seeking God is itself a social act. And if God's Love has gone into action in This World in the Redemption of mankind of Christ, then Man's efforts to make himself liker to God must include efforts to follow Christ's example in sacrificing himself for the redemption of his fellow men. Seeking and following God in this way that is God's way is the only true way for a human soul on Earth to seek salvation. The antithesis between trying to save one's own soul by seeking and following God and trying to do one's duty to one's neighbour is therefore wholly false. The two activities are indissoluble. The human soul that is truly seeking to save itself is as fully social a being as the ant-like Spartan or the bee-like Communist. Only the Christian soul on Earth is a member of a very different society from Sparta or Leviathan. He is a citizen of the Kingdom of God, and therefore his paramount and all-embracing aim is to attain the highest degree of communion with, and likeness to, God Himself; his relations with his fellow men are consequences of, and corollaries to, his relations with God; and his way of loving his neighbour as himself will be to try to help his neighbour to win what he is seeking for himself—that is, to come into closer communion with God and to become more godlike.

If this is a soul's recognised aim for itself and for its fellow souls in the Christian Church Militant on Earth, then it is obvious that under a Christian dispensation God's will *will* be done on Earth as it is in Heaven to an immeasurably greater degree than in a secular mundane society. It is also evident that, in the Church Militant on Earth, the good social aims of the mundane societies will incidentally be achieved very much more successfully than they ever have been or can be achieved in a mundane society which aims at these objects direct, and at nothing higher. In other words, the spiritual progress of individual souls in this life will in fact bring with it much more social progress than could be attained in any other way. It is a paradoxical but profoundly true and important principle of life that the most likely way to reach a goal is to be aiming not at that goal itself but at some more ambitious goal beyond it. This is the meaning of the fable in the Old Testament of Solomon's Choice and the saying in the New Testament about losing one's life and saving it.

Therefore, while the replacement of the mundane civilisations by the world-wide and enduring reign of the Church Militant on Earth would certainly produce what today would seem a miraculous improvement in those mundane social conditions which the civilisations have been seeking to improve during the last six thousand years, the aim, and test, of progress under a truly Christian dispensation on Earth would not lie in the field of mundane social life; the field would be the spiritual life of individual souls in their passages through this earthly life from birth into This World to death out of it.

But if spiritual progress in time in This World means progress achieved by individual human souls during their passages through This World to the Other World, in what sense can there be any spiritual progress over a time-span far longer than that of individual lives on Earth, and running into thousands of years, such as that of the historical development of the higher religions from the generation of Abraham to the Christian era?

I have already confessed my own adherence to the traditional Christian view that there is no reason to expect any change in unredeemed human nature while human life on Earth goes on. Till this Earth ceases to be physically habitable by Man, we may expect that the endowments of individual human beings with original sin and with natural goodness will be about the same, on the average, as they always have been as far as our knowledge goes. The most primitive societies known to us in the life or by report provide examples of as great natural goodness as, and no lesser wickedness than, the highest civilisations or religious societies that have yet come into existence. There has been no perceptible variation in the average sample of human nature in the past; there is no ground, in the evidence afforded by History, to expect any great variation in the future either for better or for worse.

The matter in which there might be spiritual progress in time on a time-span extending over many successive generations of life on Earth is not the unregenerate nature of Man, but the opportunity open to souls, by way of the learning that comes through suffering, for getting into closer communion with God, and becoming less unlike Him, during their passage through This World.

What Christ, with the Prophets before Him and the Saints after Him, has bequeathed to the Church, and what the Church, by virtue of having been fashioned into an incomparably effective institution, succeeds in accumulating, preserving and communicating to successive generations of Christians, is a growing fund of illumination and of grace— meaning by "illumination" the discovery or revelation or revealed discovery of the true nature of God and the true end of man here and hereafter, and by "grace" the will or inspiration or inspired will to aim at getting into closer communion with God and becoming less unlike Him. In this matter of increasing spiritual opportunity for souls in their passages through life on Earth, there is assuredly an inexhaustible possibility of progress in This World.

Is the spiritual opportunity given by Christianity, or by one or other of the higher religions that have been forerunners of Christianity and have partially anticipated Christianity's gifts of illumination and grace to men on Earth, an indispensable condition for salvation—meaning by "salvation" the spiritual effect on a soul of feeling after God and finding Him in its passage through life on Earth?

If this were so, then the innumerable generations of men who never had the chance of receiving the illumination and grace conveyed by Christianity and the other higher religions would have been born and have died without a chance of the salvation which is the true end of man and the true purpose of life on Earth. This might be conceivable, though still repugnant, if we believed that the true purpose of life on Earth was not the preparation of souls for another life, but the establishment of the best possible human society in This World, which in the Christian belief is not the true purpose, though it is an almost certain by-product of a pursuit of the true purpose. If progress is taken as being the social progress of Leviathan and not the spiritual progress of individual souls, then it would perhaps be conceivable that, for the gain and glory of the body social, innumerable earlier generations should have been doomed to live a lower social life in order that a higher social life might eventually be lived by successors who had entered into their labours. This would be conceivable on the hypothesis that individual human souls existed for the sake of society, and not for their own sakes or for God's. But this belief is not only repugnant but is also inconceivable when we are dealing with the history of religion, where the progress of individual souls through This World towards God, and not the progress of society in This World, is the end on which the supreme value is set. We cannot believe that the historically incontestable fact that illumination and grace have been imparted to men on Earth in successive installments, beginning quite recently in the history of the human race on Earth, and even then coming gradually in the course of generations, can have entailed the consequence that the vast majority of souls born into the world up to date, who have had no share in this spiritual opportunity, have, as a result, been spiritually lost. We must believe that the possibilities, provided by God, of learning through suffering in This World have always afforded a sufficient means of salvation to every soul that has made the best of the spiritual opportunity offered to it here, however small that opportunity may have been.

But if men on Earth have not had to wait for the advent of the higher religions, culminating in Christianity, in order to qualify, in their life on Earth, for eventually attaining, after death, the state of eternal felicity in the Other World, then what difference has the advent on Earth of the higher religions, and of Christianity itself, really made? The difference, I should say, is this, that, under the Christian dispensation, a soul which does make the best of its spiritual opportunities will, in qualifying for salvation, be advancing farther towards communion with God and towards likeness to God under the conditions of life on Earth, before death, than has been possible for souls that have not been illuminated, during their pilgrimage on Earth, by the light of the higher religions. A pagan soul, no less than a Christian soul, has ultimate salvation within its reach; but a soul which has been offered, and has opened itself to, the illumination and the grace that Christianity conveys, will, while still in This World, be more brightly irradiated with the light of the Other World than a pagan soul that has won salvation by making the best, in This World, of the narrower opportunity here open to it. The Christian soul can attain, while still on Earth, a greater measure of Man's greatest good than can be attained by any pagan soul in this earthly stage of its existence.

Thus the historical progress of religion in This World, as represented by the rise of the higher religions and by their culmination in Christianity, may, and almost certainly will, bring with it, incidentally, an immeasurable improvement in the conditions of human social life on Earth; but its direct effect and its deliberate aim and its true test is the opportunity which it brings to individual souls for spiritual progress in This World during the passage from birth to death. It is this individual spiritual progress in This World for which we pray when we say "Thy will be done on Earth as it is in Heaven." It is for the salvation that is open to all men of good will—pagan as well as Christian, primitive as well as partially civilised—who make the most of their spiritual opportunities on Earth, however narrow these opportunities may be, that we pray when we say "Thy Kingdom come."